# The Complete Scuba Diving Guide

Dave Saunders

In the same series:

# The Complete
# Scuba Diving Guide

Dave Saunders

with

photography by
Mike Portelly

A & C Black · London

*For Michael*

First published in 1987 by
A & C Black (Publishers) Limited
35 Bedford Row
London WC1R 4JH

Saunders, Dave
    The complete scuba diving guide.
    1. Scuba diving
    I. Title
    797.2'3        GV840.S78

    ISBN 0-7136-5536-4

ISBN 0 7136 5536 4

### Photographic credits

All photographs by Dave Saunders, except
the following:

Mike Portelly: cover photograph and those
on pp. 3, 6, 7, 10, 115 (bottom), 118, 119
(bottom), 122, 130, 134 (top right), 135

Fran Saunders: pp. 26, 35, 38, 54, 83, 86,
87, 90 (bottom), 95 (top)

### Acknowledgements

My special thanks go to Kendall McDonald,
Colin Blackman, Mike Portelly, Martin and
Marian Benson and Colin Burgess for their
help in preparing this book.

Printed and bound in Great Britain by
Hazell Watson & Viney Ltd, Aylesbury, Bucks.

# Contents

# Introduction

A scuba diver is someone special. He has joined a select minority who have had the privilege of experiencing the underwater world at first hand. He has learned to cope successfully in an environment for which Nature has not equipped him. A good diver is someone who can combine his adventurous, independent spirit with a reliable and selfless approach to his sport.

Thanks to television documentaries and feature films, millions of people have been introduced to the idea of scuba diving. Many have dreamed of swimming through shoals of multicoloured fish or exploring coral reefs and ancient wrecks. Yet few know what it really feels like to be weightless. Few have fed fish by hand, or watched marine life at close quarters.

No film, however good, can ever prepare you for the real sensation of scuba diving. As you slip beneath the surface, all sound recedes except the hissing intake of breath and the bass gurgle of expelled air bubbles. You descend slowly, your senses tingling. You know that diving is a risk sport and the element of danger adds to the excitement — but the risk is a calculated one.

Exploring a coral-encrusted wreck.

Some fish can be hand-fed.

with a cylinder of compressed air after just a brief period of instruction. This partly accounts for the success of many tropical holiday resorts which invite newcomers to 'have a go'. And what an opportunity! With the minimum of tuition, you can put on all the gear and follow the instructor below the surface.

And that's fine, as long as nothing goes wrong. However, there are still some disreputable operators who are more interested in your money than your safety. They will take chances with your life, and so inevitably will push up the accident rate.

Also, if the introduction to diving is a magical experience which runs like clockwork, some people

A novice diver goes down for the first time.

Now that reliable and sophisticated equipment is available, the underwater world has become safer, more comfortable and more accessible than ever before. It is no longer only the hardy adventurers who are learning to share the exhilaration of diving. People from all walks of life are deciding to take the plunge.

The emphasis of any training should be on survival through the use of safe equipment and correct diving procedure. The details of training courses offered by different diving organisations vary, and some are better than others. This book covers both the theory and practice of good diving in a variety of conditions, and should be used to supplement practical training sessions with a competent, qualified instructor.

## Early considerations

Almost anyone who is fairly confident in water can go down

imagine that this 'taster' in warm, clear tropical waters makes them a fully fledged diver, able to cope with anything. But they have only dabbled in the sport, and dabblers are not divers. What if they knocked their mask off underwater or became tangled in a fishing line or ran out of air?

A diver is someone who knows what is going on and can act accordingly. He understands the theory and can put it into practice. If you don't know what the dangers are, how can you minimise them?

The taster should be viewed simply as a stimulus to prompt you to take a full training course with a recognised organisation. No reputable dive shop or dive centre will refill your air cylinder or allow you to hire their equipment unless you are suitably qualified, or are accompanied by an instructor. Chapter 3 makes it clear what could happen to someone foolish enough to ignore the rules.

Membership of a diving organisation may include third party liability insurance cover.

Make sure you are also covered for equipment loss or damage.

At first, the amount of information you need to know to become a diver may seem overwhelming. But take it step by step, building on your knowledge. And don't worry if you feel uncertain in the early stages. Most people are a little anxious when they start diving, and this is quite natural. In most cases an eagerness to experience the sport will overcome any apprehension, and confidence will increase as you progress.

# 1. How diving developed

About seventy per cent of the earth's surface is covered with water, about a million cubic miles of it! Most of the sea bed can be reached only by deep water submersibles, but the fringes of the oceans rise to a depth which is within the grasp of the ordinary man or woman. Divers can explore the underwater world in relative safety, as long as they understand how to go about it.

Man has always been intrigued by what lies below the surface of the ocean, and has devised many ingenious ways of probing the concealed depths. His main problem has been how to breathe underwater. Today our technology and understanding of the physical principles involved make it sound easy, but there is still much to learn about how best to manage the marine environment.

It all began thousands of years ago, when people held their breath and dived to gather shellfish, mussels and oysters for food. In Mesopotamia (the area that is now Iran and Iraq) there is evidence of divers 6,500 years ago. Later, people went down for pearls and sponges, often free-diving deeper than 20m (66ft) to find the best specimens.

Some 300 years BC Aristotle described a rudimentary diving bell. This large inverted container was heavily weighed down and

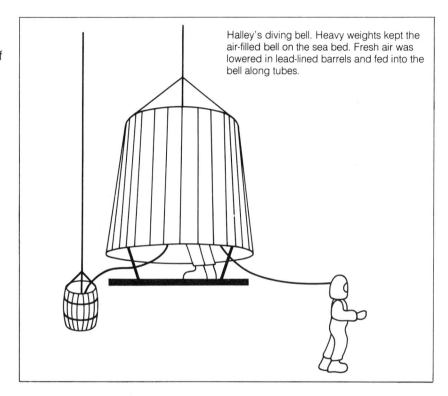

Halley's diving bell. Heavy weights kept the air-filled bell on the sea bed. Fresh air was lowered in lead-lined barrels and fed into the bell along tubes.

lowered into the water, with air trapped inside. The diver could use the bell as a base from which to work, until the level of carbon dioxide became too high.

There are stories of divers using breathing tubes to stay down for long periods. But this was only effective just below the surface, because the increased pressure on the chest made it very difficult to expand the lungs enough to inhale the air in the tube when submerged

more than about 45cm (18in). This is why a very long snorkel is ineffective.

The British scientist and astronomer, Dr Edmund Halley, improved the diving bell by sending down 160 litre (36 gallon) barrels of fresh air, which were released under the bell to replenish the supply. In 1690 Halley himself remained in the bell for 90 minutes at a depth of 18m (60ft). Halley also devised individual bells which

'diving engine', and looked through a glass port-hole. His arms protruded through specially sealed holes in the side, enabling him to salvage loot from wrecks.

A hundred years later John Deane was the first to use a diving helmet. Deane's original helmet was refined and became the standard method of undersea exploration for nearly a hundred and fifty years. Modern versions are still used today by commercial divers. Encased in a watertight suit and weighed down with lead-soled boots, the diver was lowered to the bottom where he could walk around slowly. Air was pumped down an umbilical tube into his helmet which had glass port-holes so he could see what he was doing.

Diving is safe if you keep to the rules.

divers wore on their heads; these had breathing tubes which linked them with the main bell.

The principal interest at this time was in salvaging wrecks, and many different inventions and modifications appeared. One of the more successful ones was designed by John Lethbridge in Devon, England. In 1715 he constructed a rigid wooden tube 1.8m (6ft) long and 0.8m (2.5ft) in diameter, tapering towards the feet. Lethbridge lay inside the tube, or

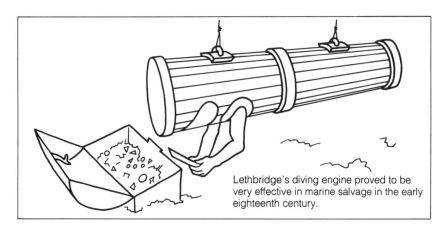

Lethbridge's diving engine proved to be very effective in marine salvage in the early eighteenth century.

In addition to marine salvage, divers were called on for repair and construction work. Financial profit provided the main motivation for the improvements made to diving equipment. Without this impetus, it is doubtful whether diving purely for pleasure would ever have attracted the great following it enjoys today.

During the nineteenth century several new designs emerged from England, America and France, incorporating a reservoir of

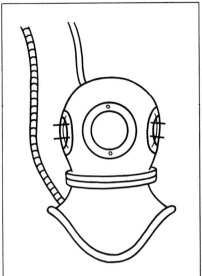

A modified version of Deane's diving helmet was used for a century and a half. The diver was linked by rope to an attendant on the surface. Air was pumped down a tube into his helmet.

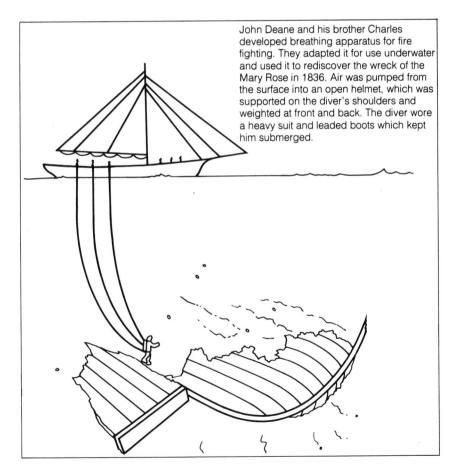

John Deane and his brother Charles developed breathing apparatus for fire fighting. They adapted it for use underwater and used it to rediscover the wreck of the Mary Rose in 1836. Air was pumped from the surface into an open helmet, which was supported on the diver's shoulders and weighted at front and back. The diver wore a heavy suit and leaded boots which kept him submerged.

compressed air, or 'lung'. In 1865 two Frenchmen, Rouquayrol and Denayrouze, developed the first regulator. It was located between the metal canister of compressed air and the breathing tube. A valve regulated the amount of air the diver received, and a membrane allowed for changes in pressure as he descended or ascended. Pressure in the canister was maintained by pumping air down from the surface.

However, at the time, cylinders that were light enough to use were not strong enough to hold air at sufficient pressure for deep dives. The diver was still attached to the surface by his air-line, which was needed to replenish his supply.

Development of the aqualung or Self-Contained Underwater Breathing Apparatus (SCUBA) marked the beginning of sport diving in its present form.

the regulator and strong air cylinders, the stage was set for the advent of sport diving as we know it today. It was only fifty years ago that Jacques Cousteau, then an officer in the French Navy, was working on a system that was to enable a diver to swim relatively freely underwater, like a 'manfish', independent of heavy boots and copper diving helmet. During World War II, while military frogmen were involved with sabotage and demolition, Cousteau was thinking more constructively. In 1943, together with engineer Emile Gagnan, Cousteau produced the aqualung or Self-Contained Underwater Breathing Apparatus (SCUBA). His cylinder was filled with compressed air and had a regulator or demand valve which automatically dispensed air on demand at the ambient pressure.

After the war, the aqualung was marketed throughout the world. Diving was promoted as a sport which was available to the non-professional enthusiast. With the alluring attraction of books and films by Hans Hass and Jacques Cousteau, scuba diving soon became the fastest growing sport in America, and, during the 1960s and '70s, the fastest growing sport in the world. Many diving clubs were established where people could use the equipment and obtain the necessary instruction.

This problem was overcome in 1900 when Louis Bouton produced a compressed air cylinder which could cope with nearly 200 bar (2,900 psi).

With the further development of

# 2. Equipment

Human beings are not designed to exist underwater: we are clumsy and slow-moving, and our eyes are not equipped to see clearly. But most important, our bodies cannot extract life-giving oxygen directly from the water. An individual needs to take with him a variety of 'props'. The basic equipment includes:

- snorkel to help him breathe while swimming on the surface
- mask to help him see underwater
- fins to help him move more fluidly
- cylinder to supply the air when underwater
- regulator to enable him to breathe the air from the cylinder
- contents gauge to tell him how much air there is in the cylinder
- wet suit to keep him warm
- dry suit to keep him warmer
- weights to keep him down
- lifejacket to keep him up
- depth gauge to tell him how deep he is
- watch to tell him how long he has been down
- knife to cut him out of an entanglement
- compass to help him navigate
- torch to illuminate underwater objects

These are the basic tools of the trade. Diving is all about using them correctly and safely. If they are not all familiar to you at this point, don't worry, they soon will be...

The total amount of scuba gear which is considered to be the basic requirement seems daunting at first. Yet, once you appreciate the significance of each item, it all appears more manageable.

To save continuous repetition, the following terms will be used: *regulator* for demand valve or DV; *contents gauge* for air pressure gauge; *air cylinder* in preference to tank or bottle; *harness* rather than backpack; and *aqualung* for harness, cylinder and regulator together as one unit. The glossary on page 142 contains a more complete list of diving terms.

This chapter will introduce all the basic equipment. It will describe the function and design of each item, then point out what to look for when making a purchase. Besides the information given here, a good dive shop assistant should be able to give you specific, detailed advice on the variety of equipment available. Having read this chapter, you will be able to arm yourself with

In order to survive underwater for any length of time a diver needs a range of props.

all sorts of questions to fire. Don't be afraid to ask searching and even awkward questions: it is your money and your safety that you are protecting, so don't let the assistant get away with not telling you the limitations of various models. You *need* to know. If he does not know the answers, find someone who does. Do not just buy the equipment because you want to use it on a dive planned for the next day.

## Snorkelling gear

Swimmers who find keeping afloat a tiring struggle will welcome the freedom provided by mask, snorkel and fins. Such simple aids enable you to float or swim effortlessly on the surface of the water without the need to keep lifting your head for a gasp of air.

### Snorkel

Because you lose buoyancy when you raise your head above the surface, it is much less of a burden if you leave it *in* the water. Although breathing then naturally becomes a problem, a snorkel soon releases you from this predicament.

Snorkels can be either 'J'- or 'L'- shaped, with a mouthpiece that you grip *gently* between your teeth. Most are made of heavy duty rubber and should ideally have bright orange luminous tape

retaining loop is made of flexible rubber

A snorkel enables a surface swimmer to keep his head down and continue breathing. It can be attached to the mask with a retaining loop.

around the top so that they can be seen easily. On surfacing after a duck dive, or if water splashes into the tube, you can clear it with a short, sharp blow. Some modern snorkels have valves which make it easier to blow water out of the tube when you surface. This is because most of the water is dispelled through the valve and does not

have to be pushed right to the top of the tube.

When in use the snorkel is attached to the mask strap by a retaining loop, or is slipped between the mask strap and your head. When using scuba gear, the snorkel is not needed and can be hung around the neck on a cord, or strapped to the leg.

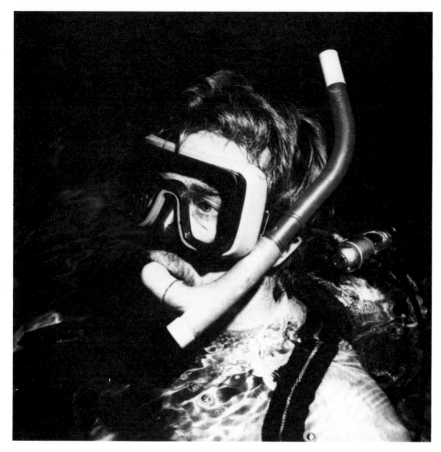

## Mask

A mask keeps water away from the eyes so that vision is not impaired. However, there is still a slight distortion: light is refracted as it passes through the faceplate, making objects appear closer than they really are (see chapter 3).

The mask should have a double seal to keep out the water and a soft nose pocket so you can pinch your nose when clearing your ears (see chapters 3 and 4). All masks should have tempered toughened glass which is usually replaceable if the glass becomes cracked. Masks

A valve in the bottom of this snorkel makes the job of expelling water much easier because it does not have to be forced up the whole length of the tube.

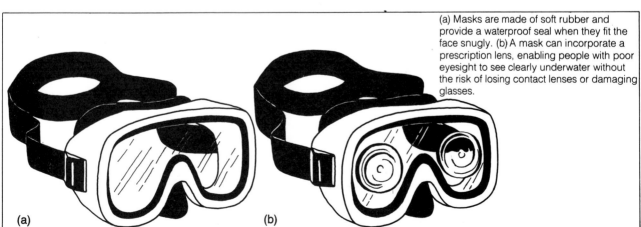

(a) Masks are made of soft rubber and provide a waterproof seal when they fit the face snugly. (b) A mask can incorporate a prescription lens, enabling people with poor eyesight to see clearly underwater without the risk of losing contact lenses or damaging glasses.

(a)          (b)

Specs with 'armless' frames can be clipped into the mask.

are sometimes made of non-allergic silicone rubber. Some models have a drain valve in the nose pocket, so you can blow out the water, but the technique of mask-clearing, described in chapter 4, is now generally preferred.

To test if the mask is a good fit, hold it against your face and breathe in gently through your nose. The vacuum created by extracting some of the air will keep a well-fitting mask in place even when you take your hand away. If it is a poor fit, gaps around the seal will let in air and the mask will fall off.

People who normally wear glasses or contact lenses can get a prescription mask made. Alternatively, some opticians sell 'armless' frames which clip into your existing mask. These can be taken out and used in another mask if, for example, you buy a new one.

## Fins

Fins enable you to move faster and more easily while in the water, but trying to walk on land with them is about as graceful as a penguin with cramp!

When wearing fins underwater you seldom bother to use your arms to propel your body forwards. Arms are inefficient compared with the thrust provided by the fins, and they generally remain loosely by your sides, or, if it is cold, folded across your chest. The powerful force exerted by the fins does the majority of the work of moving and steering you. Arms are sometimes used when manoeuvring,

especially in a confined space.

Fins come in a variety of designs. Some have a strap around the ankle, others have a pocket which the foot slots into. An extra

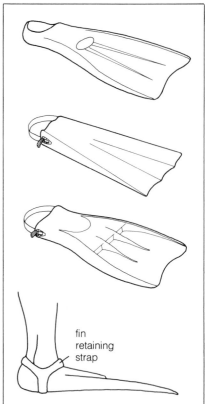

fin
retaining
strap

Several different designs of fin are on the market. The type with a built-in heel can be held in place more securely with a retaining strap.

16

restraining strap may be used to hold the fin on.

Jet fins have a large surface area and incorporate vents which direct the flow of water and reduce unnecessary effort. Vents just below the toes allow water to flow through the fins when bringing the foot up, thereby reducing the resistence and making finning easier. They increase forward propulsion as opposed to upward lift, and call for less effort on the up-kick.

Stiffer fins with a larger surface area require greater strength to manoeuvre them. Larger fins mean you work harder, but go further for each fin stroke. If you have weak leg muscles, don't imagine you'll turn yourself into Superman by wearing large fins!

A compressor pumps normal air into SCUBA cylinders.

# SCUBA gear

Since air is not freely available underwater, it is obviously the main element that divers have to take down with them. Devising a system which enables them to do this successfully was the turning point in underwater exploration. The development of Self-Contained Underwater Breathing Apparatus (SCUBA) in the 1940s marked the beginning of sport diving as it is known today.

## Aqualung

Think of the aqualung as having three parts to it: the harness or backpack, the cylinder and the regulator.

The harness consists of adjustable straps, worn like a rucksack, attached to a clamp which holds the cylinder. The waist strap should have a quick release buckle so it can be removed easily.

The cylinder is filled with air, *not* with oxygen. In order to have enough air to last for more than just a few minutes the cylinder is filled with *compressed air*. As this air is under pressure, it should be treated with care. In a full cylinder the air pressure might be between 200 bar (about 3,000 psi) and 238 bar (about 3,500 psi).

Although different countries have different legal requirements, markings on the cylinder should give details of most of the following: the manufacturer, the date of manufacture, the date of the last test, cylinder capacity, maximum pressure to which it can safely be filled and the weight of the cylinder. These markings should be clearly visible.

The compressor which pumps in the air has at least two filters to prevent water vapour and impurities from entering the cylinder. Although an individual can cope with small amounts of

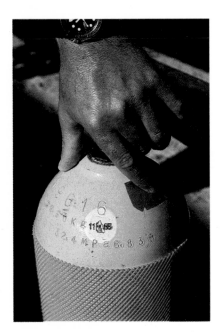
Markings on the cylinder indicate when it was last tested.

When the on-off tap (red) is on the top of the pillar valve it has to be small so that the regulator 'A' clamp can fit over it.

pollution in the air breathed, this can become highly toxic under pressure in concentrated form (see chapter 3).

Scuba cylinders come in different sizes, ranging from 1,133 litres (40 cu ft) to 3,483 litres (123 cu ft). They are made of either aluminium or steel. Aluminium is much less susceptible to corrosion than steel, but it is a softer metal and is therefore more vulnerable to damage.

At the top of the cylinder is the

pillar valve. Many American and European cylinders are fitted with a 'J' valve. The 'J' has a so-called air

reserve of about 20 bar (about 300 psi). A spring-operated restrictor reduces the flow of available air at 20-25 bar, so the diver is alerted to the fact he is running short of air. He then releases the reserve by

A twin set is two cylinders mounted together. This one has an octopus rig (a double regulator) for use in emergencies when a fellow diver runs out of air.

before descending, or it could be knocked on inadvertently. Then when it becomes hard to breathe and he tries to pull the reserve, there will be no more air available. At 30-40m this can be a real problem. It is infinitely better to monitor your air supply constantly by checking the air contents gauge.

The 'K' valve is a simpler design and there is less to go wrong. With no misleading 'reserve', there is less chance of an accident due to diver error.

Some pillar valves have an on/off tap on the top. Because the regulator has to be fitted over this tap, the tap has to be quite small and therefore may be difficult to turn on or off. A cross-flow valve avoids this problem by locating the on/off tap on the side. As the regulator is attached to the orifice at the top, the knob for the tap can be large and easy to operate.

Twin sets, that is two cylinders mounted side by side, are heavier and bulkier to carry about, but they do provide more air, which is especially useful when you come on to decompression dives.

pulling a rod, which runs down the side of the cylinder.

The commonest problem with the 'J' valve occurs when the diver presumes that his 'J' valve is on. In reality he can forget to check it

## Regulator

The air in the cylinder is under pressure. You could not possibly breathe it directly from the cylinder. It is the job of the regulator to control the amount of air you

When the on-off tap is on the side of the pillar valve it can be larger and easier to manipulate because the regulator does not go over it.

receive; it slows it down to a manageable level. The regulator, or demand valve, enables the diver to breathe at depth by supplying him with air 'on demand' at the pressure of the surrounding water.

It is a simple, robust, but remarkably effective, piece of equipment. A typical modern single hose regulator has two valves, or stages, which reduce the air pressure. These are connected by

20

a medium-pressure flexible rubber hose.

The first stage is attached to the pillar valve by means of an 'A' clamp, with an 'O' ring to ensure an airtight seal. The first stage reduces the air pressure from the pressure of the cylinder to about 6-10 bar above ambient pressure.

The second stage reduces the pressure to that of the surrounding water. Besides the mouthpiece, this section has a purge button and exhaust vents for expelled air. It contains a diaphragm with water

on one side of it, and an air space on the other. When you breathe in, you suck out the small amount of air from this space, thus causing the diaphragm to bulge in towards your mouth. This activates a lever which releases air from the tube into the chamber for you to breathe. Thus you are supplied with air 'on demand'. As soon as you stop breathing in, the diaphragm returns to its flat position and the lever shuts off the air supply. Because the diaphragm is deflected according to the

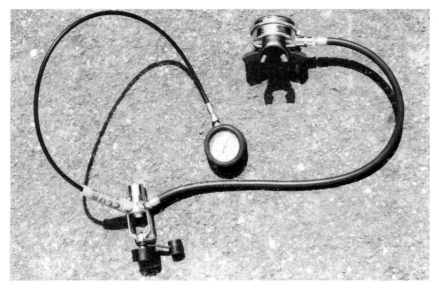

The regulator or demand valve is attached at one end to the compressed air cylinder and has a mouthpiece at the other end. It has two valves or stages which reduce the pressure of the air in the cylinder to ambient pressure.

Information on these aspects of regulators is very scanty. Try to press the retailer to find out more from the manufacturer about the limitations of each model.

### Octopus rig
If a diver runs out of air, or if his regulator develops a fault, he can share his diving buddy's, or companion's, air supply using the

pressure of water on it, you always breathe air at the same pressure as the surrounding water.

Better quality regulators are more efficient and reliable. Cheaper ones are more likely to present problems when delivering air below about 30m. Drawing air from some regulators becomes difficult at lower cylinder pressures, and with less sophisticated models, it is possible to 'beat the lung' if you demand air more rapidly than the regulator can supply it.

When your safety depends on the reliability of the equipment, as it does with a regulator, go for one of the well-known makes. Although no guarantee against failure, it does improve the odds.

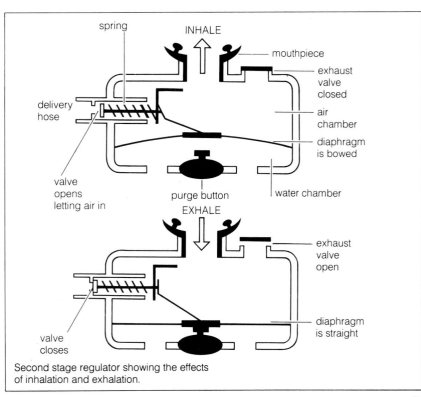

Second stage regulator showing the effects of inhalation and exhalation.

The contents gauge gives an indication of the amount of air left in the cylinder.

method described in chapter 4. However, it is much easier if an octopus rig is used. This is a 'spare' second stage, which can be used if your buddy's regulator fails, or if he runs out of air.

### Contents gauge
The first stage has a number of ports which provide air for different uses. As seen earlier, the first stage supplies air to the second stage and, if used, to the supplementary octopus rig.

Upstream of the valve, which reduces the cylinder pressure, is a hose leading to a contents gauge. When the air supply tap is turned on, air from the cylinder fills the hose and the gauge indicates the pressure of the air in the cylinder. This gives an indication of the

amount of air left. When the cylinder is a quarter full, it is time to ascend. This level is sometimes indicated by a red or shaded zone on the gauge.

To prevent it swinging loosely, the pressure gauge can be tucked through the neck of your lifejacket or through a harness strap.

Downstream of the valve, in the medium pressure section, other ports may supply the direct feed line to your lifejacket (see page 29) or a dry suit inflation hose (see page 24).

### Cylinder accessories
A plastic mesh may be used to protect the surface of the cylinder against scratches, and to separate it from metal parts of the harness. Paint on the cylinder also helps protect it. A rubber 'boot' cushions the base of the cylinder when it is put down in an upright position.

## Diving suits
When submerged in water the body loses heat very quickly, yet it is vital that you keep your body core warm at all times, especially in the area of the kidneys either side of the small of the back. In water colder than about 20°C (68°F) a diving suit is needed to restrict the amount of heat you lose. During a long or deep dive, even in tropical waters, protection from exposure is usually necessary. And besides the chill factor, the suit gives protection from knocks and scratches.

### Wet suits
Wet suits are made of neoprene foam, containing numerous little gas (nitrogen) bubbles. Nowadays the neoprene is usually sandwiched between nylon linings which protect it from scuffing, and is more comfortable on the skin.

Wet suits come in a variety of designs. You can get separate trousers, jacket, hood, gloves and bootees. Or the hood might come attached to the jacket. Long johns are a similar shape to dungarees, and they protect your kidneys better than wet suit trousers. A shortie wet suit for warm waters extends down to just above the knees, and has short sleeves.

As neoprene is buoyant, you will be more buoyant in a full wet suit than a shortie one. The version you choose depends on personal preference and the temperature of the water in which you are most likely to be diving.

Wet suits let water in through the neck, cuff and ankle openings. In contact with your body, this trapped water then warms up and provides a thin insulating layer. When buying a suit, go for one which is as closely fitting as possible, while still allowing adequate freedom of movement. Great gaps allow too much water to move about, and the warm water will simply be flushed out.

A wet suit 7mm thick will be warmer than one which is only 3mm, but you will lose out on flexibility. Windsurfers and water skiers tend to wear thinner wet suits which give greater flexibility because they are not totally submerged for as long as a diver. These suits may be suitable for divers in warm locations, but in cooler waters most divers prefer to accept a loss of agility in favour of the comfort of being relatively warm.

Divers with an average shaped body will probably be able to buy a wet suit off the peg. If you cannot find one which fits snugly, it is worth considering having one tailor-made.

With safety being a major factor, you should also consider selecting gear with a conspicuous colour.

Diver wearing a membrane dry suit.

White shows up best against a dark background because it provides a good contrast. On the other hand, black shows up best when looking up towards the surface, which is lighter. Many divers feel that black is the most appropriate colour for a diving suit, whereas any item which should be visible from the boat when the diver reaches the surface, should be as bright as possible — a fluorescent orange hood, for example.

### Dry suits

The great advantage of a dry suit is that it is warmer than a wet suit. This is why they are used extensively in commercial diving, and have only recently come into vogue among sport divers. Apart from your face, hands and sometimes feet, water does not come into contact with your body. As a result, you can wear dry clothes next to your skin. But there are other factors to consider. A dry suit has its own inherent problems, and calls for additional training to appreciate the different ways in which it behaves.

There are two types of dry suit — the variable volume or foam neoprene dry suit, and the cheaper, lighter-weight, but tough membrane suit. Normally the suit is one-piece, though sometimes the bootees and hood are separate. There is a 'dry' hood with a face seal, or a wet hood which allows water to come into contact with your head. Each type of suit has a method of inflation. Some have dump valves, a number of which are manual, whereas others are automatic.

Because air is trapped inside the suit, you need to wear more weights than you do with a wet suit to keep you down while in the water.

Although the air in the suit adds insulation, which helps keep you warm, it creates great buoyancy changes at different depths. The air is compressed as you descend, making you become less buoyant

Fitting the direct feed line which supplies air from the cylinder to inflate the dry suit.

An automatic dump valve on this dry suit can be set to the required level of buoyancy. On ascent, expanding air will be released through the valve.

(see chapter 3). To compensate for this the diver can control the amount of air in the suit. It is this method of buoyancy control which complicates the use of a lifejacket and makes additional instruction necessary.

Check the inflation and venting operation *before* entering the water to make sure that they work, and that you have a good seal. During descent, air can be added by pressing a button or turning a tap on the inflation valve or inlet tube, which leads from the first stage of the regulator to the upper chest of the suit.

When swimming down head first, air can collect in the legs or boots of the suit, making it very difficult to

control your position. Some divers wear small ankle weights to help stop air flowing into their boots and to keep their feet down. However, it is probably simpler to have a dry suit which is fairly close-fitting around the lower half of the body.

On ascent, when the air in the suit is expanding, a press-button exhaust or dump valve can be opened to vent excess air. If you do not do this, you risk a rapid ascent and the possibility of a burst lung or decompression sickness (see chapter 3). In order to vent air from a suit in the event of dump valve failure, slip a finger into a wrist seal, hold your arm up and make an opening large enough to release air from inside the suit. An automatic dump valve can be set to whatever level of buoyancy you want. Air will then be automatically vented according to the changes in pressure.

One of the hazards of dry suits lies in the danger of flooding due to zipper failure. Besides losing buoyancy and the advantage of being *dry*, your soaked clothes will add to your weight and make leaving the water more difficult.

When buying a dry suit, there is little point going for a tailor-made model because having a perfect fit is not as important as it is with a wet suit. A dry suit needs to be loose-fitting enough to wear clothing underneath. This creates more drag while swimming along, but only becomes tiresome when you want to swim long distances.

### The neoprene dry suit
The variable volume or neoprene dry suit is made of 6mm or 8mm thick neoprene, which is usually sandwiched between nylon linings. It is warm, comfortable and easy to use.

You enter the suit through an opening, often in the upper back, which is then sealed with a sturdy waterproof zip. The zip, neck and wrist seals should be lubricated with talcum powder before use, to help the suit slide on more easily. The seals should be turned in on themselves, making a closer fit. The

Neoprene dry suit.

suit needs some air in it for the neck seal to work properly.

### The membrane dry suit
As a membrane suit is made of thinner, lighter-weight material — butyl/nylon laminate — it is not as warm as the neoprene suit, and you need to wear something underneath. A purpose-made 'woolly bear' suit, made of polyester acrylic fibre, is a more efficient alternative to a track suit, or slacks and a pullover when extra warmth is needed.

The latex seals around the neck and wrist are a weak point of this type of dry suit, and can tear. Treat them carefully. On a dive holiday take spare seals and specialised glue (see manufacturer's recommendation).

The warm 'woolly bear' suit is worn under a membrane dry suit.

### Weights and weight belt
Divers wear weights, or blocks of lead, to keep them submerged. A nylon or rubber belt is threaded through holes in the blocks and worn around the waist.

As the air in the lungs makes a diver buoyant, and as some of the equipment is buoyant, he would never get below the surface if he did not carry weights. Wearing lead weights compensates for this buoyancy and enables a person to dive. A correctly weighted diver should be able to hang suspended underwater, without sinking or surfacing.

Because we are all built differently *and* are likely to be

Weights threaded on a weight belt are worn around the waist to enable the buoyant diver to remain below the surface.

Buoyancy compensator (BC) showing the $CO_2$ cartridge.

wearing different amounts of neoprene, each individual needs to wear different amounts of weight. So don't expect to use exactly the same weight as the next diver.

Different weights will also be needed for diving in different conditions. Salt water, for example, is denser than fresh water, and a diver will be more buoyant in salt water and will therefore need about 2 kg more weight.

Divers should weight themselves according to the conditions, rather than put on a standard amount of weight each time, then use the lifejacket to compensate for differences due to clothing or water density changes.

If a diver gets into difficulty underwater and needs to surface,

he can ditch the weight belt and will immediately become more buoyant. Because of its use in emergencies, it is essential that the belt can be released quickly and easily. You should be able to find and operate the quick-release mechanism by feel, even with gloves on.

## Lifejackets and buoyancy aids

There are times when your lifejacket can be your greatest friend. It can give you buoyancy when you need it at depth, it can help bring you to the surface and it can support your weight while you are on the surface.

All divers should wear a lifejacket, even if they have a dry suit and can control buoyancy by inflating and venting the suit. Several types of lifejacket or

buoyancy aid are available, but they are not all suitable for divers.

### Surface lifejacket (SLJ)
The SLJ is for use on the surface and is not adequate for the needs of the diver. It contains a small carbon dioxide ($CO_2$) cartridge which can be used *once only* to inflate the jacket in an emergency. It can also be inflated orally. This type of jacket may be used by the boat-handler or by snorkellers, but would be ineffective at depth

because the $CO_2$ would not fill the jacket when under pressure.

Another problem with a cartridge that can be used only once is that you cannot be sure it will work. You can compare its weight with a full cartridge to confirm that the $CO_2$ has not leaked, but even if you keep it clean and free from corrosion, there is always the chance that it may not function when you need it.

The cartridge is activated by pulling a cord. This cord must be pulled at the right angle if the cartridge is to be properly punctured by the firing pin. The action is made difficult because the cartridge is often hidden behind a flap or in a pocket.

### Buoyancy compensator (BC)

BCs are used to adjust buoyancy, to bring a diver up in an emergency and to provide support on the surface.

Some BCs are fitted with a $CO_2$ cartridge, others have a direct feed leading from the main cylinder, and some can be inflated orally. The $CO_2$ cartridge is for use only on the surface. The direct feed relies on the main cylinder for its supply of air, and is therefore of no use in an

BC showing the direct feed which supplies air from the main cylinder to the jacket.

The adjustable buoyancy lifejacket has a small cylinder of compressed air which can be tested before you enter the water.

emergency resulting from an empty cylinder.

An integral BC and cylinder is popular in America, although it means that the cylinder cannot be jettisoned without also forfeiting the jacket. This type of BC is not a true lifejacket because it will not turn a

body upright on the surface and support it face up.

### Adjustable buoyancy lifejacket (ABLJ)
The ABLJ is the most suitable type of lifejacket for the diver. Unlike the SLJ and BC, the adjustable

buoyancy lifejacket has its own separate rechargeable cylinder of compressed air. This small cylinder is usually housed in a sleeve at the base of the ABLJ. It contains sufficient air to inflate the jacket fully at depth, which a $CO_2$ cartridge cannot do. Thus the ABLJ can be used in an emergency to lift the diver to the surface as well as give him support while waiting for the rescue boat. The jacket is designed to hold an unconscious diver in an upright floating position with his face exposed.

Prior to the dive a small cylinder is filled with compressed air from the main cylinder. It is then attached to the ABLJ and can immediately be tested to make sure it is functioning correctly. The ABLJ can also be inflated orally via a hose which hangs down the side of the jacket. When adjusting buoyancy underwater, it is easier to use the small cylinder. But avoid making frequent adjustments, so as to save the compressed air for use in case of an emergency.

The mouthpiece on the end of the oral inflation hose can be used to breathe air *from* the ABLJ in an emergency. If a diver is trapped — in a fishing net, for example — he can partially inflate his ABLJ from the small cylinder of compressed air, and breathe in this air via the oral inflation hose. However, this technique should be used only as a

Adjustable buoyancy lifejacket (ABLJ).

last resort because it is difficult to carry out in moments of stress.

Some ABLJs are fitted with a direct feed as well, which enables the diver to control buoyancy using air from the main cylinder.

Air can be vented by pulling the toggle which operates the dump

Inflated ABLJs ease the job of towing an exhausted diver to safety.

valve at the top of the jacket. In some cases this valve also acts as an over-pressure valve which lets air escape when the jacket is over-
30

inflated. Other jackets have a separate over-pressure valve. You can also vent the jacket by holding up the oral inflation hose and pressing the button which opens the valve.

Most ABLJs are equipped with a whistle to attract attention on the surface.

### Depth gauge
The depth gauge is an essential item of dive equipment. To dive safely you need to know your

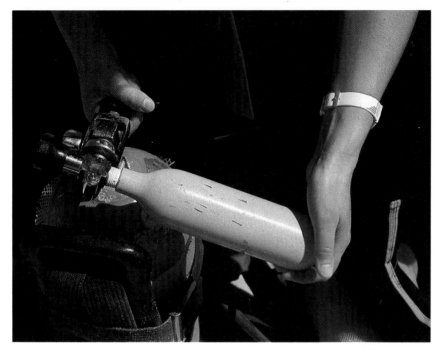

The ABLJ has its own small cylinder of compressed air which is filled from the main cylinder.

It is important that the depth gauge is accurate to within a small margin of error. If the gauge registers that you are shallower than you really are, you will be running the risk of going deeper than you have allowed for. This will increase your chances of suffering from the bends (described in chapter 3). For the sake of a metre or two, it is always best to allow yourself an extra margin for safety.

Unfortunately, even some new gauges are inaccurate, and therefore dangerous. You should

depth and the length of time you have been underwater. You need to know these accurately in order to use the dive tables illustrated in chapter 6, and to avoid the hazards of diving too deep.

The depth gauge is worn like a watch around the wrist, or as a part of a console of gauges. Some consoles incorporate a dive timer, a knife, dive tables, a slate and waterproof pen. The depth gauge has a calibrated scale which indicates your depth below the surface. On some models the markings are luminous so they are easy to read underwater in poor visibility.

Inserting the small cylinder in the ABLJ.

A depth gauge. It is essential to know your depth during a dive in order to stay within the safety limits.

compare your gauge with those of fellow divers, and have it recalibrated if necessary. It's a good idea to do this from time to time anyway, as the accuracy of the gauge may deteriorate after being knocked about in a dive bag for a season or two.

There are two main types of gauge, the capillary and the bourdon tube. The capillary gauge comprises a tube of air which is open to the water at one end. As depth increases, the air in the tube is gradually compressed by the pressure of water. It is compressed to half its volume within the first 10m, to a third of its volume at 20m, and to a quarter of its volume at 30m. Thus the scale along the tube becomes smaller with depth. By reading off the position of the air

bubble, you can see how deep you are. The capillary gauge is more useful in shallow water, as the divisions are well spaced out. But, the deeper you go, the more difficult it becomes to take an accurate reading of the smaller divisions.

The bourdon tube is a curled tube which unwinds or straightens under pressure, depending on the type of tube. Different tubes are filled with oil, water or air.

### Dive computer
Some manufacturers are experimenting with decompression computers. The more ambitious models do most of the following: indicate the depth, indicate the pressure in the cylinder, time the dive, time the surface interval, indicate maximum allowable depth, time repeat dives and indicate ascent rate. A light or alarm warns

the diver when it is time to surface.

Impressive new technology has its place in diving, but it does not make you a better diver. Don't expect a console of digital readouts to do away with the need for constant monitoring of conditions and events. Good equipment should supplement good procedure, not replace it.

### Dive watch
As chapter 3 will illustrate, you cannot dive as deep as you like for as long as you like. Nor can you simply stay down until the air runs out, and then surface, without first calculating that it is safe to do so. You must keep within certain limits to minimise the risks of an accident.

A dive watch, or timer, is one of the essential tools which enable you to keep within the bounds of safety. By knowing how long you have been below the surface, you can make sure that you stay within the recommendations of the dive tables and avoid problems associated with the effects of water pressure on your body. The maximum depth and duration of the dive should be agreed before each dive. A watch enables you to keep to your dive plan and co-ordinate your movements with the dive boat or dive marshal on land.

The watch should be water resistant to a depth of 90m; it

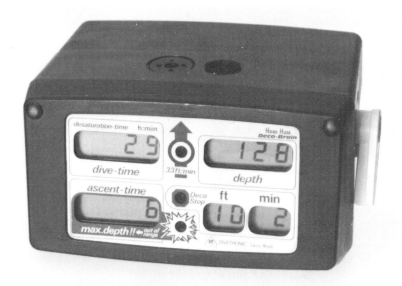

This dive computer detects the change from air to water. It constantly monitors changes in pressure, and automatically adjusts dive times, decompression stops, ascent rate and surface interval times.

The strap for the watch or timer should be made of strong rubber, plastic or stainless steel. A steel strap is more likely to catch on an item of equipment, but can be worn under the wrist of your glove. Leather straps deteriorate fast in water.

### Dive knife

A good knife is an important — and easily lost — item of dive gear. Besides being useful for anything from cleaning your finger nails to peeling oranges, a knife can save your life if you get caught in a fishing net underwater. Some modern nets are made of nylon

set the planned length of the dive: it starts automatically when you begin a dive, then sounds an alarm when your time is up.

should have a luminous face, which can be read easily, even in murky water. It should have a moveable bezel around the watch face, with click stops which can be set to the position of the minute hand at the beginning of the dive. Avoid a watch with a bezel that moves too readily, as it may inadvertently be moved off its original setting.

Some digital watches have a stopwatch button which should be easy to press with a gloved hand.

Using a dive timer you can pre-

A dive watch should be easy to read in poor visibility, and should have a rotating bezel which can be set to the time the dive began.

A dive timer gives more information than a watch and is activated when it enters the water.

monofilament, like a fishing line, and they are designed *not* to break.

Dive knives come in all shapes and sizes, with prices to match. So what should you look for when choosing a knife? Ideally, you want one with a corrosion-resistant blade, usually of stainless steel. The handle may be made of steel, hard rubber, plastic or resin. A metal butt end is useful as a hammer or to attract attention by knocking it against your cylinder.

Choose a knife with a double-sided blade, with serrations on one edge. This can be used on strong materials where a sawing action is

needed. Be wary of knives with sharp points — you may stab yourself. Some knives have a sharpened angled notch (a line-cutter) that is ideal for freeing yourself from nylon line.

Whether you choose a pointed or chisel-shaped blade depends on what you intend to use it for. A chisel-end is best for prizing things off, while a sharp point makes a good 'stabber'.

Many knives have a scale marked on one side of the blade.

The sheath or scabbard should incorporate a locking mechansim, so you do not lose the knife when swimming down or finning hard. It can be strapped to your arm or leg or, in some cases, screwed to a gauge console. Some dry suits

incorporate a knife pouch as an optional extra, usually on the outside of the thigh.

**Compass**
On a dive you may try to stick to a rigid course — 15 minutes in one direction, then 15 minutes back again. But what about currents sweeping you off course? Or the fact that you may have a tendency to swim to the left or the right because one leg may be stronger than the other?

If visibility is good, you may be able to pick out certain landmarks, but what if there is nothing very distinctive? To save yourself all this doubt, include a compass in the equipment you take down with you. Wear the compass either on a

lanyard around the neck, or on the wrist. You can then take a bearing holding it in front of you with both hands, or reading the compass like a watch. Be sure to hold it in the same position each time you check your course.

The compass must be resistant to pressure. Ideally it will be oil-filled, and have a needle that does not jam readily.

The points of the compass should be easy to read, with a clearly marked direction-of-travel line. Choose a compass with a rotating bezel which can be aligned with Magnetic North. You will then be able to see if you are deviating from your pre-set course.

### Torch

Water absorbs light and the deeper you go, the more colours are filtered out. Reds are the first to go. Below about 10m red appears black and the undersea environment takes on an almost uniform green-blue appearance. A torch will enable you to see the true colours of reef, rocks or marine life.

During the day a torch is a useful extra. At night it is essential, and night dives should not be attempted without a good torch in the hands of *each* diver.

A dive knife is kept in a sheath which should have some method of preventing it from falling out.

A compass should have a rotating bezel which can be set on any bearing.

In murky water, containing a lot of plankton, or where the sediment has been stirred up, a torch beam is as effective as car headlights in fog. The beam merely reflects off the particles in the water, and visibility is not improved.

There is a wide choice of torches, from the large and powerful to the cheaper, smaller models. They are, of course, resistant to water pressure. Most come with a strap which can be looped around the diver's wrist. Some are turned on by tightening the bulb section into the body of the torch, others have a switch.

36

## Accessories
- *Log book* to record dives and have any tests signed up.
- *Maps* of the coastline and *charts* of the waters in which you intend to dive.
- *De-humidifier*, instead of spit, to clear your mask.
- *Slate* on which to write messages underwater. This can simply be a piece of roughened perspex.
- *Pencil* to write with.
- *Goodie bag* in which to collect underwater treasures.
- *Close-up lens attachment* mounted on the outside of the mask gives a three and a half times magnification. Useful for close inspection of marine life, or to help people with poor eyesight to read gauges, watch or camera settings.
- *Specialist gear* for underwater photography, archaeology etc. (see chapter 8).

## Spares
- straps for mask and fins
- extra weights
- silicone grease for regulator or torch seals
- 'O' rings for pillar valve on cylinder

## Dive bag
The prospect of keeping all your gear together can become a real problem unless you have a sturdy, water-resistant dive bag. This holds all your gear, except cylinder and harness, and may be made of strong nylon.

## Small medical kit
Each dive bag should contain a few basic first aid items for minor ailments (a larger first aid box should be within easy reach to serve a group of divers):

- clearly labelled waterproof box or bag
- first aid book
- adhesive dressings
- cotton wool
- cotton crêpe bandage - 8mm (3in) wide
- safety pins
- scissors
- tweezers with fine points
- triangular bandage
- antiseptic cream
- lip cream
- sun screen
- Aspirin
- butterfly stitches
- eye drops

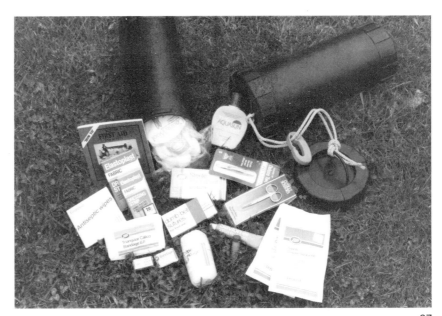

First aid boxes used by divers should have watertight seals.

A crêpe bandage is slightly elastic and will shape around and support an injured limb. Butterfly stitches are an easy-to-use substitute for conventional stitches.

### Large medical kit
Besides the items listed above the main first aid box should include:
- thermometer
- rescue, exposure or survival bag
- a range of prepared sterile dressings (a thick pad with attached bandage)
- a roll of zinc oxide plaster 25mm x 5m
- 4 triangular bandages

A survival bag may be a very large plastic bag. A diver suffering from exposure should climb inside the survival bag or wrap himself up in the rescue blanket to keep in as much body warmth as possible.

## Care and maintenance of gear

It is worth looking after your gear for two reasons: it will last longer and, more importantly, it is less likely to fail you at a critical moment.

Dive equipment performs better with regular use. Frequent

Keep most of your gear together in a dive bag.

servicing is especially important for regulators, valves and lifejackets. Failure to check and service your gear frequently is like neglecting to service a car — sooner or later something will fail, possibly with fatal results.

You should be able to maintain most of your own gear. This keeps down costs and helps you understand the inner workings of the equipment. It does not apply to the inspection and cleaning of the interior of the cylinder, or major maintenance of the regulator. Give these jobs to someone who is properly equipped and qualified.

The *cylinder*, *regulator* and *ABLJ cylinder* should be taken for regular testing. Cylinder testing is governed by national regulations which vary according to the standard of design. The strength of the cylinder walls should be checked, rust or corrosion dealt with, valves cleaned and 'O' rings replaced. The cylinder should then be washed in fresh water and thoroughly dried.

If the air pressure in the cylinder is allowed to fall very low during a dive, salt water can enter it via the regulator and may cause serious problems. Corrosion can eat away at the walls of the cylinder and can weaken it considerably, with the resulting danger being that of an explosion.

Never store a steel cylinder

which is completely empty, as moisture from the air can seep in and cause corrosion. The cylinder should be left containing 3 or 4 bar (about 50 psi). This is less important for an aluminium cylinder as aluminium is less prone to corrosion, but it is still good practice to help prevent any impurities from entering the cylinder.

Steel cylinders should be stored in a vertical position so that the corrosive effect of any water inside is not spread over a large area. Corrosion is accelerated under increased oxygen partial pressure (see chapter 3). When a cylinder is full, the partial pressure of oxygen is high and therefore corrosion is encouraged. The process of corrosion uses up the oxygen in the cylinder. It has been known for a diver to die because of lack of oxygen in just 4m of water, although his contents gauge indicated his cylinder was full. The cylinder had been stored full for several months with a small amount of corrosion inside. This corrosion fed on the oxygen in the cylinder, leaving an oxygen deficiency.

All cylinders should be washed down frequently, as they may suffer electrolytic corrosion at the point of contact between the cylinder and the stainless steel or brass harness clamp.

Chlorine in swimming pools

attacks neoprene, while the salt in sea water corrodes metal buckles, zippers, etc. All gear should therefore be rinsed out with fresh water after you have finished diving for the day. Even if you have been diving in a fresh water river or lake, a good rinse will clean out any mud, weeds, etc. which can degrade the material.

Keep an eye on the metal *zippers* of diving suits, dive bags etc. An occasional squirt of light oil will keep them rust-free. If they do become slightly corroded, dip a wire brush or tooth brush into vinegar and scrub it. When it is clear, rinse the zip thoroughly in fresh water.

After rinsing your *knife* in fresh water, and removing touches of rust with fine steel wool, that too can be sprayed with a light oil. The serrations and line-cutter can be sharpened with a small file, and the bevelled edge can be sharpened using an oil stone.

Rubber under tension tends to crack. Remove straps from *masks* and *fins* when storing them for long periods.

When storing your *wet suit*, coat the rubber surface with a fine layer of plain talcum powder. This prevents the surfaces sticking and so minimises the chances of the rubber rotting.

*Dry suits* should be rinsed with fresh water after use. A neoprene

All dive gear should be rinsed in fresh water after use.

dry suit is heavy, and the material will become distorted if hung up. It is better to lay it out on a clean, flat surface. A good dry suit should last five or six years, with frequent use.

During normal use water can get inside your *lifejacket*. To drain this out, first inflate the jacket, turn it upside down so the vent hole is at the bottom, then open the vent and squeeze the jacket so the air rushes out taking the water with it. This is more effective than simply opening the drain hole and letting the lifejacket drain on its own.

After a dive open your *torch* and take out the batteries. Check for evidence of water. Corrosion from salt water will considerably shorten the life of your torch.

Buying gear secondhand is perfectly acceptable as long as it is in good condition and 'in test'.

## Checklist of equipment
- ○ dive bag
- ○ swimming costume
- ○ towel
- ○ log book
- ○ snorkel, mask, fins
- ○ cylinder, harness, regulator
- ○ contents gauge
- ○ diving suit, bootees, gloves, hood
- ○ weight belt and weights
- ○ lifejacket
- ○ depth gauge
- ○ dive watch
- ○ dive knife
- ○ compass
- ○ torch
- ○ spare straps and weights
- ○ silicone grease
- ○ pillar valve 'O' ring
- ○ medical kit
- ○ maps, charts
- ○ goodie bag
- ○ slate and pencil

- ○ underwater cameras, etc.
- ○ windproof anorak (boat dive)
- ○ warm clothing
- ○ talcum powder
- ○ hand cream for dry skin after the dive
- ○ high energy food and drink
- ○ money, including coins for phone calls

## Dos and don'ts
*Do*
- ○ ask a lot of questions when buying dive gear
- ○ learn how to use the equipment properly, then practise using it
- ○ look after your gear
- ○ keep cylinders in test at all times
- ○ check you take all necessary gear with you on a dive
- ○ rinse all gear after a dive
- ○ replace any medical supplies at the first opportunity

*Don't*
- ○ skip this chapter
- ○ buy dive gear in a hurry and without researching it
- ○ dive with faulty or out-of-test equipment
- ○ fold up your diving suit or lifejacket when storing it
- ○ hang up a neoprene dry suit
- ○ try to carry out major maintenance work on the cylinder or regulator
- ○ store cylinders empty

# 3. Physical laws and their effects on divers

You do not need a degree in physics to dive safely, but it *is* necessary to understand a few of the basic principles related to diving.

Many of these principles come into play as a result of the pressure of water which is exerted on a diver when he dives. Water pressure affects the body and dive equipment in a number of ways. It is important to appreciate what is going on in order to make diving easier and more fun, and to avoid accidents. Some of the physical laws may sound complicated at first, but are, in fact, quite straight forward.

## Pressure

When you are underwater the water exerts a pressure on you. It is not only pressing down on your head, but also exerting a pressure on your body from all sides. As you descend, the water pressure, or hydrostatic pressure, increases rapidly with depth. Because the human body is largely made up of water and solids, water pressure has little direct effect on it. But it does have a marked effect on any air that goes down with the diver. If you take an inflated balloon underwater, the air will be compressed into a smaller and smaller volume, and the balloon will shrink, as the pressure increases.

Then, when you surface, the pressure decreases and the volume will increase again.

The physicist named Boyle was the first to show the effect of water pressure on gas (air). *Boyle's Law* states that when the pressure is doubled, the volume of the gas is halved, and vice versa. The need to understand Boyle's Law will soon become clear.

At sea level the atmosphere exerts a pressure which is measured as 1 bar or 1 atmosphere. This is equivalent to 14.7 lb per square inch (psi). At 10m (33ft) below the surface of the water, this pressure is doubled to 2 bar (29.4 psi). For each additional 10m down the pressure is increased by another bar or atmosphere.

Imagine an upturned bottle or glass which, at the surface, is full of air. At 10m, where the pressure is 2 bar, the air in this bottle will have been compressed into just half its original volume (see diagram on p.42). At 20m, where the pressure is 3 bar, the bottle will be a third full of air. At 30m, 4 bar, a quarter full, and so on.

The change in the volume of air is more marked nearer the surface. The volume is halved in the first 10m of water, whereas between 40m and 50m the amount by which the air is further compressed is very small.

In the same way, any parts of your body or equipment which contain air, such as the lungs, will be compressed as you descend (see the diagram of the collapsing bottle). So, to enable your lungs to expand normally, you need to supply them with air at the same pressure as the surrounding water,

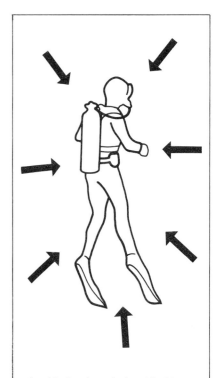

An object underwater is subject to pressure from all sides. This pressure increases with depth.

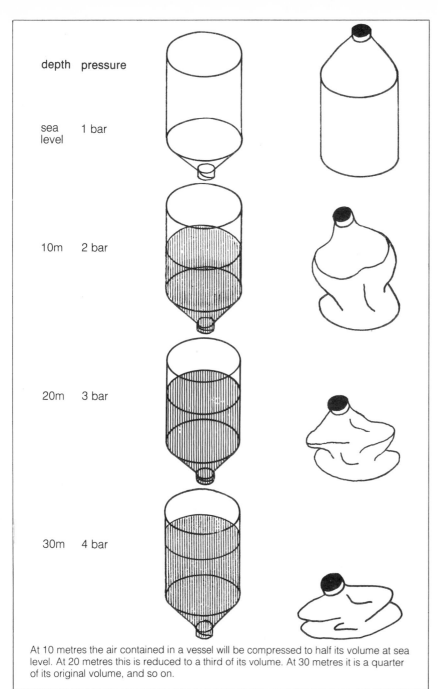

depth  pressure

sea level  1 bar

10m  2 bar

20m  3 bar

30m  4 bar

At 10 metres the air contained in a vessel will be compressed to half its volume at sea level. At 20 metres this is reduced to a third of its volume. At 30 metres it is a quarter of its original volume, and so on.

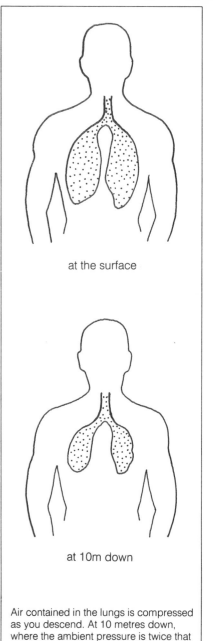

at the surface

at 10m down

Air contained in the lungs is compressed as you descend. At 10 metres down, where the ambient pressure is twice that on the surface, air in the lungs will be reduced to half its volume at the surface.

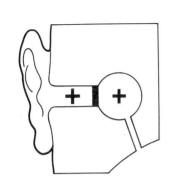
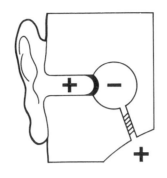

The effects of pressure on the ears. Normally the pressure either side of the eardrum will be equal. As a diver descends, water pressure forces the eardrum to flex inwards, causing pain. This imbalance of pressure can be equalised by opening the eustachian tube and letting in air from the throat/ nasal cavity.

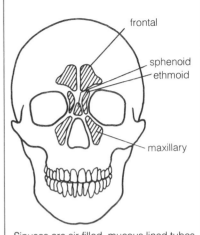

Sinuses are air-filled, mucous-lined tubes and cavities in the bony tissue of the skull.

that is, with *compressed air*. It is the job of the regulator to supply the air at the same pressure as the surrounding water.

As you go deeper, the air you breathe is denser or more compressed. You will therefore get through your supply much quicker at depth. At 20m, for example, you will breathe three times more air than at the surface; at 30m you will use four times as much air as on the surface.

### Pressure on ears and sinuses

As you descend the air in your inner ear decreases in volume, again creating a slight vacuum, which sucks in the eardrum. When this happens you must equalise the pressure either side of your eardrum by opening your eustachian tubes which link the inner ear to the nasal cavity. Some people can do this just by swallowing, others hold their nose and blow gently. This technique is described and illustrated in chapter 4 (p.58).

The sinuses are a collection of air-filled tubes and cavities in the head, which normally only give trouble when you have a bad cold or flu. If you have difficulty clearing ears or sinuses, you should not dive.

### Other air spaces

As you dive down the air in your mask is also compressed, and the resulting mini-vacuum causes the mask to squeeze against your face. Compensate by breathing out slightly through your nose into the mask.

There is gas in the fabric of your wet suit as well. As you descend, this is compressed and the volume is decreased (see diagram on p. 44). Similarly the air in your lifejacket is compressed as you descend, and expands as you ascend.

### Released pressure

This is the second part of Boyle's Law: as pressure *decreases* the volume of air *increases*. Remember the balloon? As you go up, the pressure will lessen. The volume of air will double between 10m (2 bar) and the surface (1 bar). Just imagine if a diver takes a lung full of air at 10m, and then surfaces without releasing any. The volume of air will double and he will most likely burst a lung. Thus Boyle's law explains why it is vital not to hold your breath while ascending.

### Burst lung

There are three kinds of burst lung,

43

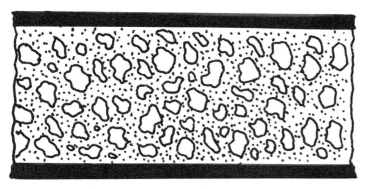

normal

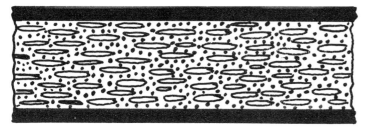

under pressure

The insulating capability of a wet suit decreases with depth because the nitrogen within the fabric is compressed under pressure.

underwater. This air will expand as you ascend and you will need to belch.

Small pockets of air in tooth cavities may give you problems if the expanding air cannot escape. If this is painful you will have to have the filling attended to.

On the same principle, the air in your wet suit and lifejacket will expand as you surface. The amount it expands depends how deep you are. Rising from 50m to 40m, the amount of expansion will be relatively small. But during the final 10m of the ascent the volume of air will double. The significance of this will become apparent when considering Archimedes' Principle.

## Buoyancy

*Archimedes' Principle* states that an object submerged in water experiences an upward force equal to the weight of the water it has displaced.

Think of the upward force as buoyancy, and the diver as the object immersed in the water. The water gives the diver buoyancy ... otherwise he would plummet to the bottom.

Lungs can hold up to 6 litres of air when full and about 1.5 litres when breath has been fully expelled. Some of this capacity can be used to increase or decrease

defined according to where the air goes when it ruptures the lung lining:
1. An *air embolism* occurs when the air enters the blood stream and forms bubbles. These can cause a blockage which prevents the movement of oxygen around the body. If this stops the heart muscles, the result will be a heart attack. If the brain is deprived of oxygen, brain damage or death may result.
2. *Emphysema* is the result of air entering the tissues between and

above the lungs, and may cause the base of the neck to swell.
3. *Pneumothorax* occurs when the air finds its way into the area between the lungs and the chest wall (the pleural cavity).

A diver with a burst lung is likely to be dizzy, numb, or paralysed and will have difficulty breathing. The treatment for a burst lung is dealt with at the end of this chapter.

### Other expanding air
It is possible to swallow air into your stomach while you are breathing

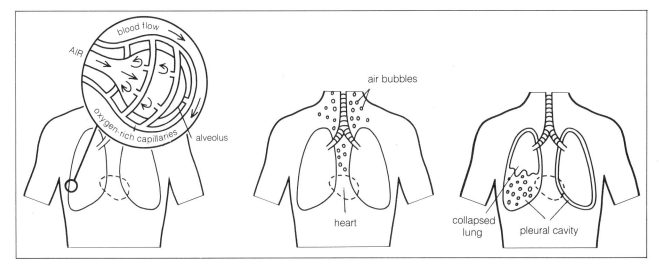

Three types of burst lung. (a) Air embolism. The exchange of air in the lungs takes place in the alveoli. These tiny air sacs are embedded in a mass of capillaries. If the alveoli are forced to expand too much they will tear, allowing air bubbles to escape into the blood stream.

(b) Emphysema. Air released from the ruptured alveoli may travel through the passages between the lung tissue and enter the tissue around the heart between the lungs (mediastinal emphysema), or above the lungs around the neck (subcutaneous or interstitial emphysema).

(c) Pneumothorax. The lungs are contained within membranes called pleura. When air escapes into the pleural cavity it will cause the lung to collapse.

volume, and thus control buoyancy.

If a diver is correctly weighted he will normally be *neutrally buoyant*, in other words, neither rising nor falling in the water. By breathing in he will expand his lungs, thus increasing his volume. This in turn will displace a greater volume of water. The water will therefore exert a greater upthrust, making the diver more buoyant — he will become *positively buoyant*. By breathing out, the diver decreases his volume, and so decreases his buoyancy, thereby becoming *negatively buoyant*.

This is a finely tuned method of controlling buoyancy; it will only work if you are already neutrally buoyant. The effects of using your breathing to control buoyancy are quite subtle and quite slow, so don't expect to bob up and down quickly every time you breathe in and out.

**Air in the equipment**
It is not only the lungs which contain air. The effects of air in the stomach, ears and sinuses have already been demonstrated. In addition, the neoprene of the wet suit contains lots of tiny bubbles of nitrogen, and there may also be air in the lifejacket. Although it contains compressed air, the cylinder has a fixed size and does not expand and contract in response to pressure changes.

Nitrogen contained within the neoprene of a wet suit, or air trapped between a dry suit and diver, is compressed as you descend (see Boyle's Law). Thus, as you go down, your total volume decreases, you displace less water and you become less buoyant. If you are neutrally buoyant at the surface, you will be negatively buoyant at 20m or 30m, because the air in your wet suit has been compressed, reducing your overall volume. You will therefore tend to sink and will either have to fin upwards to maintain the same depth, or inflate your lifejacket slightly.

The amount of neoprene you are wearing will affect the extent of this change in buoyancy. If you are wearing a full, 6mm wet suit, hood, bootees and gloves, the difference between your buoyancy at the surface and your buoyancy at 30m will be considerable; whereas in a

45

shortie wet suit with relatively few bubbles to be compressed, the difference may be hardly noticeable.

On the other hand, as you ascend the nitrogen bubbles in the wet suit will expand and you will become more buoyant. Unless you vent some air from your lifejacket, your rate of ascent will increase as you near the surface.

Any air in your lifejacket will also be compressed as you descend, making you less buoyant. Then as you come back up to the surface, the air will expand and you will become more buoyant. Unless you counter this by venting your lifejacket, you could come up too fast. The problems associated with rapid ascents are discussed later in the chapter, under *Treating diving injuries*, pp.50-1.

### Partial pressure of gases

The air we breathe is made up of approximately 79% nitrogen (about four fifths) and 21% oxygen (about one fifth), plus very small quantities of other gases such as carbon dioxide.

At the surface, where the pressure is 1 bar, the nitrogen accounts for four fifths of this pressure, that is 0.8 of a bar. The oxygen accounts for one fifth, that is 0.2 of a bar. This proportion of the pressure is called *partial pressure*. Thus the partial pressure

46

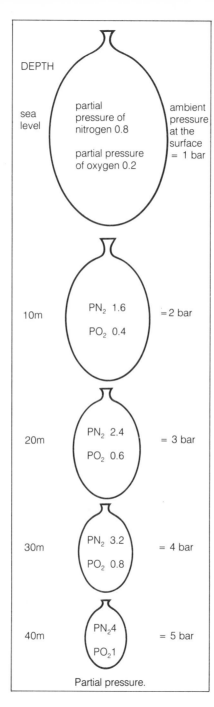

Partial pressure.

of nitrogen at sea level is 0.8 bar, and the partial pressure of oxygen is 0.2 bar.

The nitrogen and oxygen will remain the same proportion of the air when they are under pressure. As seen earlier, the regulator supplies air at ambient pressure. So, at 10m the pressure of the air breathed from the cylinder is 2 bar. Nitrogen will still account for four fifths of the total pressure at 10m, that is four fifths of 2 bar. Therefore, the partial pressure of nitrogen at 10m is four fifths of 2 bar, i.e. 1.6 bar, while the partial pressure of oxygen at 10m is 0.4 bar. At 20m the total pressure is 3 bar — nitrogen 2.4 bar, oxygen 0.6 bar. At 30m the total pressure is 4 bar — nitrogen 3.2 bar, oxygen 0.8 bar. At 40m the partial pressure of nitrogen is four fifths of 5 bar, i.e. 4 bar, while the partial pressure of oxygen is one fifth of 5 bar, i.e. 1 bar.

At a partial pressure of about 4 bar, nitrogen has a significant effect on the body — see below. *Dalton's Law* states that the total pressure of a gas equals the sum of the partial pressures of the individual gases. So, with nitrogen at a pressure of 4 bar plus oxygen at 1 bar, the total pressure is 5 bar.

Although harmless under normal surface pressure, certain gases become dangerous at the higher pressures experienced at depth.

Both nitrogen and oxygen become dangerous when their partial pressure reaches a particular level.

## Nitrogen narcosis

Deeper than 30m the concentrated nitrogen in the air supply has a partial pressure of over 3.2 bar. This can produce a condition called *nitrogen narcosis* or the 'narcs'. The diver feels slightly drunk and light-headed, hence the term *raptures of the deep*. Luckily the 'narcs' do not leave you with a hangover, but you should be wary of the effects. If allowed to continue down, the diver will lose his sense of reason and will not be able to make sensible decisions. Divers have been known to feel so happy and secure that they have taken out their regulators and offered them to passing fish! Deeper than about 60m, when nitrogen has a partial pressure of 5.6 bar, a diver's behaviour is likely to become totally irrational and he may lose consciousness.

In an extreme case, on 17 October 1943, Jacques Cousteau's colleague, Frederick Dumas, described nitrogen narcosis when he made a deep dive to 64m, well beyond the limits of the sport diver. 'I am drunk and carefree,' he reported. 'My ears buzz and my mouth tastes bitter. I have forgotten Jacques and the people in the boats. My eyes are tired ... I am

going to sleep ...' Then he returned to the surface, thinking he had only reached about 33m. 'Coming up is merry as a bubble ... the drunken sensation vanishes. I am sober.'

He was down for only seven minutes. He became more and more disorientated with depth, and the sense of elation was followed by drowsiness and increased confusion.

Professional divers planning deep dives take a mixture of helium and oxygen, rather than nitrogen and oxygen, to guard against nitrogen narcosis. It is not only nitrogen that can produce problems under pressure. Traces of carbon dioxide or carbon monoxide which may have no harmful effect on the body at the surface, can be more toxic under pressure. Hence the need to fill the cylinder with pure air.

## Oxygen poisoning

Oxygen becomes poisonous to the body when its partial pressure exceeds 1.75 bar. When using a normal mix of air, containing about 20% oxygen, you would have to dive to almost 80m before the partial pressure of oxygen exceeds this level (0.2 x 9 bar = 1.8 bar). As 50m is considered the limit of safe sport diving using ordinary compressed air, this is not a problem for the sport diver.

But if the mixture you are

breathing contains a higher concentration of oxygen, the danger of oxygen poisoning occurs earlier. This is because the critical partial pressure of oxygen, or trigger level at which oxygen becomes toxic (1.75 bar), is reached earlier. For example, if the mixture being breathed contains 40% oxygen, it will reach its partial pressure of 1.75 bar at about 37m. A diver breathing such a concentration of oxygen is putting himself at risk if he exceeds this depth. With a concentration of 60% oxygen, the limit is 21m. And with 100% oxygen the limit is only 8m. The use of oxygen and oxygen-rich breathing equipment by sport divers is not recommended, and is banned in some countries.

*Remember*: a diver breathing a normal concentration of air within safe sport diving limits will not suffer from oxygen poisoning.

## Decompression sickness or 'the bends'

The rate at which gas dissolves in liquid depends on several factors — the surface area, pressure, temperature and so on. In diving, it is important to understand the effects of pressure.

Although the air breathed contains about 80% nitrogen, the exchange which occurs in the lungs involves the absorption of oxygen rather than nitrogen.

47

However, when under pressure, some of the nitrogen also dissolves into the bloodstream and body tissues. The greater the pressure, the more nitrogen is absorbed. So the longer a diver stays down and the deeper he goes, the more nitrogen enters his system.

When he comes back up towards the surface, the ambient pressure is reduced and the reverse occurs. The nitrogen in the blood is returned to the lung surfaces and breathed out. If someone has been down to a maximum of 20m for just 30 minutes, only a small amount of nitrogen will have been absorbed into his body. This is easily dispelled when he returns to normal pressure, and no special procedure is necessary. Because you can return to the surface without stopping, this is called a non-compression or 'no-stop' dive.

But if a diver goes deep enough for long enough, a large amount of nitrogen will build up in his blood. If he then surfaces too fast, the pressure will drop rapidly and the excess nitrogen will not have time to be dispelled. Instead it forms bubbles, which become trapped in the blood and body tissues. These trapped bubbles will expand as you surface (Boyle's Law), and may block the blood circulation and even damage the nervous system. This is called

decompression sickness or 'the bends'. If the nitrogen bubbles block the flow of blood to the heart or brain, the result will be permanent injury, paralysis or death.

The risk of decompression sickness is greatly increased after a dive deeper than 50m. If, however, the diver stays within the limits dictated by the dive tables (explained in chapter 6), he reduces the risks considerably.

The tables indicate how deep you can go and for how long without needing to decompress. If you dive deeper or for longer than this limit, you will have to stop at 10m or 5m during the ascent to give the nitrogen enough time to come out of the tissues gradually.

The dive tables should be viewed as a guide, and even if you remain within the tables, it is not a perfect guarantee that you will be immune from the bends. It is always best to leave a margin for error.

Everyone's body is different. Just as alcohol affects each of us to a varying extent, so too does pressure. Some people are more susceptible to the bends than others. Overweight or over-worked divers, for example, are more likely to suffer, though it does not always follow that fitter people are more resilient in this respect. *Everyone* should stay within the safety limits.

So far, this chapter has outlined

some of the ways in which pressure can affect the body. By understanding the potential hazards, individuals can dive in such a way as to minimise the risks. The wise diver does not push his luck by over-stepping the mark.

*Charles' Law* should also be noted. This states that the volume of gas increases as the temperature increases. Imagine a cylinder or inflatable boat full of compressed air, left under a hot sun. The air inside wants to expand when it gets hotter, but, in the case of the cylinder, it has nowhere to go because the cylinder walls are fixed. In extreme cases they can explode.

This is, in fact, uncommon. It is more likely that when the cylinder is being filled, friction and the compression of air generate heat, especially if the cylinder is filled quickly. Once the cylinder has cooled down it will no longer be totally full, and there will be room for some expansion. The rubber of an inflatable boat will stretch slightly to accommodate the expanded air, and would probably develop a leak before exploding.

# Other physical laws which influence the diver's world

### Heat conduction

Water is a very efficient conductor of heat. Unfortunately, this means it conducts heat away from the diver. In waters cooler than 20°C you will need a diving suit to avoid becoming quickly chilled. Hypothermia occurs when the body gets too cold. If allowed to continue, the diver becomes lethargic, stops thinking clearly and his limbs start to feel heavy. Before reaching this stage, he should tell his buddy he feels cold by exaggerated shivering, then give the 'Ascend' signal.

### Transmission of sound

Sound is transmitted much faster in water than on land, although you cannot tell which direction it comes from. Far from being a silent world, you can hear sea creatures crunching at coral, or shingle being disturbed by wave action. A good way of attracting another diver's attention is to strike a rock or your cylinder with a stone or the butt end of your knife.

### Colour absorption

Colours are filtered out by water at different rates. First red (and orange) light is absorbed, then

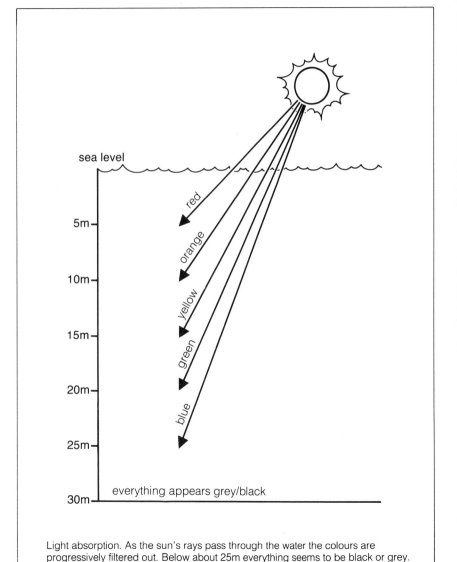

Light absorption. As the sun's rays pass through the water the colours are progressively filtered out. Below about 25m everything seems to be black or grey.

yellow, green, and finally blue. As a result, colours underwater appear muted. Even in clear water reds turn to black within 5m, and most objects look blue or green. Artificial lights are needed to bring out the colours. (See chapter 8 for the effects of light absorption on underwater photography.)

### Light refraction

Without a mask underwater vision would be extremely blurred, because human eyes have not evolved to function in contact with water. The mask traps a layer of air which enables the diver to see clearly, although with slightly distorted vision. When light passes from the water to the air space, it is refracted or 'bent'. This makes the top of a vertical object seem higher

and the bottom lower. Objects underwater appear to be a third larger and a quarter nearer than they really are. So, if something seems to be 3m away, it will really be 4m away.

## Treating diving injuries

Prevention is definitely the best cure, and diving accidents are avoided by good diving practice and regular maintenance of equipment. Serious diving injuries are rare, but nasty things *can* happen through diver error or equipment failure, and you must know what to do about them.

The cause and effects of nitrogen narcosis (the 'narcs'), decompression sickness (the 'bends') and burst lung have been

explained earlier in this chapter. But how do you treat the different conditions?

*Nitrogen narcosis* in its mild form has no after effects and requires no treatment. If symptoms become more acute, and include clumsiness, hallucinations, etc. the diver should be taken to shallow water.

*Decompression sickness* takes the form of pain in the knee and shoulder joints and muscles, pins and needles in the extremities and sometimes paralysis or loss of consciousness. Symptoms sometimes take a while to show themselves. A diver usually knows within an hour of surfacing, but the reaction may be delayed for as long as 24 hours.

If decompression sickness is suspected, the diver should be kept under close observation, and should not dive again for 24 hours. If any symptoms develop, the diver should immediately be taken to a recompression chamber. While transporting the diver, put him on his left side, with his head lower than his feet. This may help keep the bubbles away from his head and heart. Pure oxygen can be administered, if available, as this should reduce the extent of the injuries.

A recompression chamber is a pressure-proof cylinder, in which the air pressure can be regulated

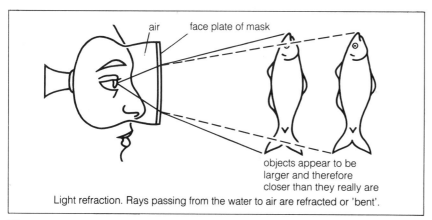

air    face plate of mask

objects appear to be larger and therefore closer than they really are

Light refraction. Rays passing from the water to air are refracted or 'bent'.

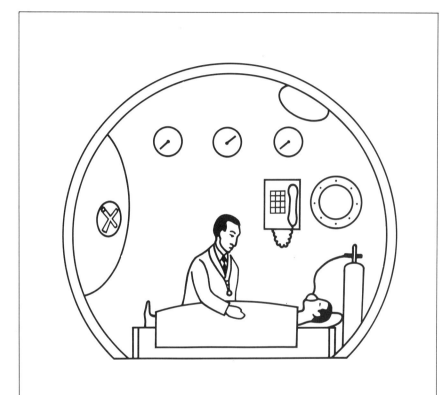

Recompression chamber. Decompression sickness or a burst lung are treated by recompressing the diver to a pressure equivalent to the maximum depth reached during the dive, and then decompressing him slowly.

communicate with the outside world. Some have an airlock which enables a doctor to enter the chamber and examine the patient.

As these chambers are few and far between and as the bends can be extremely uncomfortable, or even fatal, it is better to dive defensively, and avoid the risk of needing one.

A *burst lung* should be acted upon immediately. Speed is important. Treatment is the same as for decompression sickness. Get the injured diver to a recompression chamber as soon as possible. In the case of a burst lung it is air that has entered the blood stream, rather than nitrogen, but in both cases, recompressing the diver will recompress the bubbles — in other words, make them smaller and therefore less dangerous. Administering pure oxygen will usually help make breathing easier.

*Carbon monoxide poisoning* can cause dizziness, loss of consciousness or death. Contaminated air may have been pumped into the cylinder by a compressor with an air intake point too close to the exhaust. The best way to recover is to breathe pure uncontaminated air — not easy at 30m. Artificial respiration should be given if breathing stops.

*Carbon dioxide poisoning* is due to an excessive build up of carbon

and the patient's condition monitored. As soon as a 'bent' diver is in the chamber, it is pressurised at least up to the depth of the deepest point of the dive. This should compress the nitrogen bubbles until they disappear. Then the pressure is slowly reduced so the diver de-compresses, without the bubbles forming again. This may take several hours.

Most chambers have a bed, a glass port hole and an intercom system so the recovering diver can dioxide in the blood. It causes headaches which then lead to breathlessness and confusion. When the symptoms are detected, a diver should stop, relax and breathe steadily. If possible transfer to a fresh supply of compressed air or come to the surface for pure air.

*Hypoxia* is a shortage of oxygen. The body tissues are not receiving the oxygen they need because the diver has stopped breathing. The brain will be permanently damaged unless oxygen can be restored within four minutes. Treatment is obviously to get oxygen into the person's lungs as soon as possible. If pure oxygen is available on the surface, this will restore oxygen levels in the blood more quickly.

*Hypothermia* is a loss of body heat. The first priority is to restore this warmth. If in a warm, sheltered place, remove the wet suit and dry the person quickly with a towel and dress him in warm, dry clothes. If he is wearing a dry suit, leave it on, unless it has obviously leaked. Wrap him up in a blanket, making sure that at least one layer is underneath, or put him in an exposure or survival bag. Keep him calm and still. Give him a warm drink, but *nothing* alcoholic.

The insidious thing about hypothermia is that those in danger of suffering may not realise it; they may insist that they feel well, and try to refuse help. You have to be

firm and say it is better to wrap up warm ... just in case. Severe cases should be taken to hospital.

## Summary

o  Understanding physical laws makes diving safer, easier and more fun.

o  Within the first 10m, pressure changes are much more pronounced than at greater depth.

o  Gas will expand to twice its volume when brought to the surface from 10m, due to a decrease in pressure from 2 bar to 1 bar.

o  If you increase the volume of you and your equipment (by breathing in or inflating the lifejacket), you become more buoyant.

o  Below 30m nitrogen can produce light-headedness and hallucinations.

o  If you ascend too quickly from depth, the nitrogen dissolved in the bloodstream will form bubbles causing decompression sickness, which is usually detected by pain in the knee and shoulder joints.

o  Treatment for decompression sickness is to get the diver in a recompression chamber as soon as possible.

o  Avoid a burst lung by breathing normally during a normal ascent, and breathing out continuously during an emergency ascent.

o  A diver suffering from hypothermia may think he is fine. Be firm and insist that he gets warm and dry.

o  Oxygen poisoning is a problem only when breathing a mixture with a high oxygen concentration underwater, or going much deeper than the limit of normal sport diving.

o  If you are tired, hung-over, tense, unfit or overweight, you are more vulnerable to nitrogen narcosis, decompression sickness, exhaustion and exposure.

o  Air expands when the temperature increases. Keep full cylinders out of the sun.

o  Avoid accidents by understanding what causes them.

# 4. Pool training

As with any risk sport, it is very unwise to attempt to teach yourself scuba diving. Once your appetite has been whetted, perhaps by a 'taster' lesson while on holiday, you should enroll on a recognised training course. This might be an intensive two week course at a special diving school, or weekly training sessions with a diving club. Choose the course which suits your temperament, your cash flow and the time you have available.

In a series of lectures and practical sessions, you are introduced to the skills of diving. The emphasis is on enjoying the sport by adopting safe procedures. The rules of diving are not niceties which have been included to make the sport appear more respectable or official. They are there to minimise the risks to yourself and to fellow divers.

Ideally, the theory and practice should run concurrently. A well co-ordinated course will put into practice what you have just covered during the lectures.

This chapter covers practical training sessions which introduce you to the equipment and basic skills of diving. Training takes place in calm water, 2m - 3m deep, usually in a swimming pool.

Your course of training with a dive club may well go something like this ...

## Lesson One

### You and the equipment
After your first lesson you will be able to tell if you are cut out for diving. You will be given a good idea of what is in store, and will be able to decide if you are serious enough to go through with it. Many diving associations have a minimum age of 16 years for aqualung training.

You begin with a basic swimming test to show that you are reasonably fit and confident in the water. This involves a 200m freestyle swim up and down the swimming pool, without snorkel gear. It is not a race, and most people who contemplate learning to dive can manage this quite easily.

Now that you have warmed up, you and a small group of trainees are taken through the main items of the equipment.

You slip on your fins, first making sure that the straps are correctly adjusted. You then spit on the glass inside the mask and wipe the saliva around. This helps prevent the mask from misting up. Before fitting the mask, you rinse it out in the pool. Then, making sure that your hair is out of the way, you hold the mask against your face with one hand, and pull the strap back over your head with the other. You take hold of the snorkel, which is secured by a retaining loop, grip the mouthpiece gently between your teeth, and then slide into the water.

Careful not to breathe through your nose, you fin along the surface. When you duck dive your snorkel tube fills with water, which you clear on surfacing by tipping your head back and blowing sharply through your mouth, squirting the water out.

### Basic scuba gear
Next you take off the mask and snorkel and are introduced to some of the scuba gear. With the cylinder upright, your instructor shows you how to attach the regulator. First remove the dust cap from the pillar valve. Then slip the first stage of the regulator over the valve and, making sure that it is seated correctly, do it up hand tight.

While turning on the air tap, hold the contents gauge away from your face as there is a very slight danger, if the gauge is faulty, of the glass blowing out due to the sudden increase in pressure.

With the air supply on, put the mouthpiece in your mouth and test it out. It will feel much bulkier than the snorkel, though it is surprisingly easy to breathe through.

Check the contents gauge to ensure there is plenty of air in the cylinder for the planned dive.

After each member of the group has tried this, your instructor holds the cylinder up for you to put on the harness, which is worn like a rucksack. It weighs about 16 kg (around 35 lb), and feels it. He then adjusts the straps so that the cylinder sits comfortably on your back. Having fastened the quick-release buckle on the waist strap,

Attaching the first stage of the regulator to the pillar valve.

you put your mask on again, put the mouthpiece in your mouth and walk down the pool steps into just one and half metres of water.

With your instructor standing by, bend forwards and submerge your head in the water. At first there is a tendency to hold your breath, although you have already proved to yourself that you can get air from the regulator. But it does not take long to relax while lying face down in the water, though you are still very conscious of each breath you take.

Next the instructor explains the importance of being correctly weighted so that you are neutrally buoyant in the water (see chapter 3).

With 2kg of weight threaded onto a weight belt, you fasten the quick-release buckle. It is important that the weight belt can be ditched quickly, as that is the first item to get rid of when you want to be more buoyant.

Again you bend forwards in the water and let your legs come up behind you. This time your body sinks slowly down to the bottom of the pool and you lie there for three breaths. You are aware of the extra weight around your waist, and standing up is slightly

Check the regulator is supplying the air properly before you enter the water.

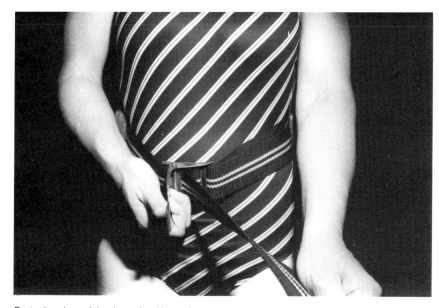

Fastening the quick-release buckle on the weightbelt.

more cumbersome than before.

You take off the weightbelt, noticing how easily the clasp comes undone, and hand it to the instructor on the pool-side. Next you undo the waist strap of the harness, slip off one shoulder strap, then the other, and pass the cylinder out to the instructor.

## Hand signals
As normal speech is out of the question underwater, hand signals make up the diver's dictionary — the language of the undersea, which must be understood by all divers.

○ The *OK* signal, given as a frequent check, is a clear 'O' made with the thumb and index finger while the other three fingers are straight and together. This means 'Are you OK?' and is also used as the reply 'Yes, I'm OK'.
○ *Not OK* or *Something is wrong* is made by placing the hand flat, palm down, and rocking it from side to side. When this signal is given, it is not an emergency but some action needs to be taken. You, or your buddy, may be having difficulty clearing your ears or perhaps some of the equipment is tangled up. This must be corrected before you continue.
○ *Help!* means that something is seriously wrong and assistance is needed immediately. It is made by waving a clenched fist, as shown in the photograph. Underwater, this is done with the elbow bent; on the surface, the arm is stretched out.
○ *Going up* or *Let's go up* is the thumbs up sign. This does *not* mean 'OK'.
○ *Going down* or *Let's go down* is the thumbs down sign, usually given at the beginning of a dive.
○ *You* or *Me* or *Let's swim in this direction* is indicated by pointing with the index finger.
○ The *Stop* signal is given by raising the palm of your hand to your buddy, like a traffic policeman's stop signal. This may be used in conjunction with 'I'm not OK', or before pointing to your watch, contents gauge or depth gauge to bring your buddy's attention to them.
○ *I'm out of breath* is shown with a back and forwards

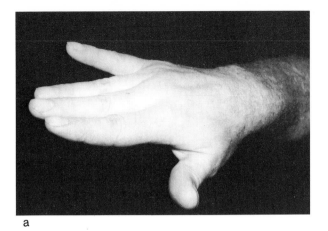

a

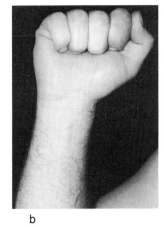

b

Hand signals.
a. Something is wrong.
   (Rock hand back and forth.)
b. Help! I'm in distress.
   (Wave fist from side to side.)
c. I'm out of breath.
d. I have no more air.
   (Chopping action to the neck.)

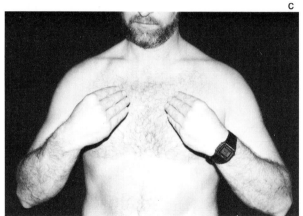

c

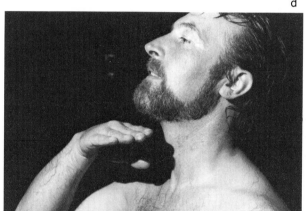

d

movement of the hands against the lower chest, indicating rapid breathing. Following this you should stop and recover.

○ *I'm short of air* is a clenched fist held still, with fingers towards your buddy. The response to this should be the 'Going up' signal to mark the end of the dive.

○ *I have no more air* is a chopping movement made with the flat hand against the throat. This situation should not arise because you should keep a constant watch on your contents gauge. If it *does* happen at depth, however, the response of the buddy is to give immediate assistance by offering his mouthpiece in order to share air.

After demonstrating the signals, the instructor conducts a question and answer session with his group of trainees to make sure everyone has a clear grasp of the signals.

### Fit to dive?

By the end of the introductory lesson, your imagination has probably been stimulated and you are eager to leap into the sea and dive to 30m! But you have a long way to go before you are ready for that. This is a time for restraint.

First you must prove that you are physically fit to dive. A medical check-up and chest X-ray will indicate if you are likely to have problems with ears, sinuses or lungs. A history of epilepsy, mental illness, asthma, heart disease, high blood pressure or diabetes may prevent you from diving. And do not dive if you are taking prescribed medication, unless you have been cleared by a doctor who understands the special conditions of diving.

It is a good idea to have regular medical check-ups. If you are younger than 30, you should have an examination every five years; between 30 and 50, every three years; and once a year after that.

### Fitness exercises
While diving itself can be very relaxing, the activities associated with it may call for considerable muscle power. Carrying heavy equipment around and diving in anything other than ideal conditions is strenuous and exhausting if you are not fit. And in the advent of an emergency, extra strength and stamina will be needed to enable you to rescue a buddy or cut yourself free from a tangled line. If you are in good physical shape, you will be better able to cope with tasks which you may be called on to perform at any time. And you will make more economic use of your air supply.

Before a dive, carry out a quick series of warm-up exercises to get the blood circulating and help keep you supple and alert during the dive, such as running on the spot and touching your toes.

## Lesson Two

### Basic manoeuvres
Having been introduced to the scuba gear, you now go back to using just mask, snorkel and fins for this lesson. The aim is to master certain basic skills.

In the deep end of the pool, where you are out of your depth, you tread water with your fins on. Keeping your legs straight, a broad scissors action keeps your head well above the surface. Next, with the addition of snorkel and mask (duly coated and rinsed), you swim along the surface, concentrating on a good finning action. With legs straight (though not rigid) and toes pointed, you move from the hips with a steady stroke.

### Duck dives
The next stage is to do a duck dive to the bottom. Before you do this the instructor checks that you know how to clear your ears and sinuses, which, even at 2m, can feel uncomfortable. Some people can clear their ears simply by going through the motion of swallowing. Others find it easier to hold the nose with thumb and forefinger, close the mouth firmly, and blow gently. Unless your

tubes are blocked, this will equalise the pressure on either side of the eardrum. If your tubes *are* blocked, because of a cold, for example, you should not dive.

The easiest way to duck dive requires the least effort. Simply float face down on the surface, then bend at the waist, so your top half is submerged. With arms pointing down, bring your legs up out of the water, keeping them together and straight. The weight of your legs will drive you under and with one arm stroke you will go down to the bottom.

To equalise the pressure on either side of the eardrum hold the nose, shut the mouth and try to force air out. This should open the eustachian tubes.

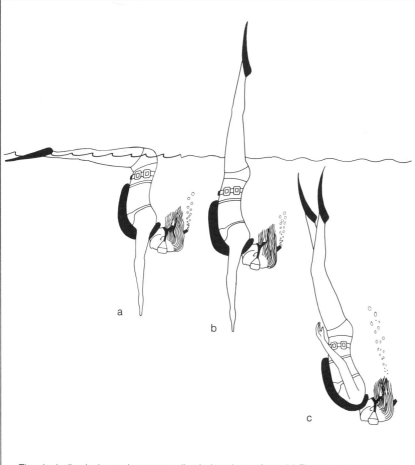

The duck dive is the easiest way to dive below the surface. (a) Float face down on the surface, bend at the waist so the top half of the body sinks down. (b) Bring the legs up out of the water so the body is straight. The weight of your legs will push you down. (c) A single powerful arm stroke will help you begin your descent; then start finning.

When at the bottom of the pool you will have noticed that your mask was pressing quite hard against your face, but that the pressure was released when you surfaced. This occurs because the air trapped inside your mask is compressed as the water pressure increases (see Boyle's Law, chapter 3). You can prevent mask squeeze by breathing out slightly through your nose.

### Keeping your cool
To become a good diver you must be confident and controlled in the water. This means keeping calm if something goes wrong. By remaining calm, you will be able to assess the situation and then decide on the most appropriate course of action. Someone who panics is likely to do something foolish. Much of the training concentrates on avoiding this unthinking response by carrying out exercises which build up confidence in yourself and your equipment.

Whenever anything goes wrong, you should correct it straight away. One thing can quickly lead to another, which may develop into a situation where you are no longer in control. If, for example, your mask is knocked off underwater, it will obviously be inconvenient, but

When you surface you should be looking up to make sure you are not about to collide with someone or something. Hold one arm outstretched above you to protect your head in case you do touch something. This is good practice for later when you will be diving in the sea. Visibility may be poor and the surface may be littered with boats, swimmers and so on.

Just before your head surfaces, start exhaling to clear the snorkel tube. Tip your head forward for the final puff to remove the water, then inhale.

you should be able to regain control of the situation quickly and with the minimum of fuss. Without a mask your vision is impaired and there is a tendency to try to breathe in through the nose. By experiencing this sensation during training, and coping with it, you are less likely to react irrationally if it happens in open water.

To help you cope without a mask underwater, and to encourage you to breathe through your mouth, you fin along the surface of the pool wearing just a snorkel, but no mask. It may take some practice before you can breathe through your mouth only, without sucking in water through your nose. But persevere.

To show that one lungful of air can last long enough to sort out most problems, hold on to the side of the pool, take a medium size breath and submerge yourself below the surface. If you take a big breath it is more difficult to hold it for any length of time. After what seems like ages, the instructor taps on your hand and you come up. 'Just over 30 seconds,' he announces.

The final exercise of lesson two is again designed to increase your confidence in a potentially hazardous situation. While treading water in the deep end of the pool you remove your mask, snorkel and fins, letting them sink

to the bottom. You then duck dive and retrieve each of these, replacing them on the surface. If you do it in more than one go, it's a good idea to pick up the mask first, as this will make it much easier to find the snorkel and fins.

## Lesson Three

### Buddy checks

From the third lesson you team up with another trainee who becomes your buddy for the duration of the course. You train as a buddy pair to get used to keeping an eye on each other and communicating by using hand signals.

Although you have your own mask, snorkel and fins, you also have access to the club's equipment. Until you buy your own gear, you are each allocated a cylinder, regulator, weight belt and weights.

Remembering what you covered in lesson one, you assemble the cylinder and regulator, and check that there is enough air in the cylinder and that the regulator is working. You then make life easier for your buddy by helping him on with his cylinder. He returns the compliment, and you check the operation of each other's waist buckle.

Next the weight belt. You each thread 2kg of weight onto your belts and fasten them. It is

especially important that you make sure you can locate your buddy's weight belt buckle, and know how it operates in case it has to be jettisoned during an emergency.

### Entering the pool

Having checked each other's gear and made sure that the air is turned on, it is time to enter the water. Standing at the pool-side, you check the water is deep enough, then insert the mouthpiece. With one hand on your mask to keep it in place, and the other hand behind you holding the cylinder to prevent the pillar valve hitting the back of your neck, you are now ready to enter the water in one of several ways:

○ by taking a long stride
○ by slipping in from a sitting position
○ using a forward roll
○ using a backward roll

The instructor enters the water first, and surfaces to watch your entry. Once in the water you come to the surface and give your buddy the 'OK' signal, then repeat the signal to the instructor.

### Buoyancy testing

With 2kg of weights, you will notice it takes more effort to tread water than without them. It's time to test your buoyancy underwater. The instructor gives the 'Going

(a)

(b)

Entering the water using (a) a forward roll and (b) a backward roll.

down' signal. At the bottom of the pool you kneel down in a small circle facing each other. The instructor points for you to go first. Lying spread-eagle on the bottom of the pool you breathe in deeply. You feel yourself lightening slightly, but it is not enough to lift you up. You get back to the kneeling position and the instructor gives you the 'OK?' signal. 'Yes, I'm OK', you reply.

Next your buddy has a go and when he breathes in, filling his lungs with air, he ascends slightly. Then he breathes out and descends again. He is correctly weighted and neutrally buoyant.

Instructor gives the 'going down' signal to two trainees.

'OK' signals all round, then 'Going up'.

As you are negatively buoyant, you tend to sink rather than stay suspended in the water, so the instructor advises 1kg instead of 2kg of weight next time.

Remember, too, that air has weight, and when air is taken from a cylinder, it becomes lighter. An almost empty cylinder with most of its air used up is about 2kg (4.4lb) lighter than a full one, so at the end of a dive you will need to compensate for this by venting some air from your lifejacket. If you are not slightly heavy to begin with, you will be too buoyant by the end of the dive because of the lighter cylinder.

Neutral buoyancy is a very relaxed, happy state to be in,

Test your buoyancy by lying spread-eagle on the bottom; as you breathe in you should slowly ascend, and as you breathe out you should descend.

because you are not constantly fighting to stay down or finning hard to prevent yourself from sinking. Don't worry if you cannot achieve this straight away; it's a technique that many people find takes time to get used to.

## Mobility

To demonstrate your control and mobility underwater, you practise forward and backward rolls. For a forward roll begin with a duck dive and immediately tuck yourself into a tight ball. Then swing your outstretched arms around together. This rotates your body in

Exchanging the 'OK' signal underwater.

a neat roll which leaves you upright on the bottom.

For the backward roll, you again duck dive, but this time,

instead of curling yourself into a ball, extend your neck, arch your back and bend your legs. Now try to swing your arms evenly so you bring your body round to the upright position once more. First attempts at the backward roll tend to be more clumsy and several tries should be made.

## Mask clearing

Clearing your mask can also take some getting used to, and needs practice. If you are lucky you will have a mask which fits perfectly and does not leak. However, it is important to know how to clear

Forward roll.

later be reduced to one good long blow.

The instructor repeats the exercise with both of you, but this time removes the mask completely and holds it at arm's length. Everything is controlled and composed. You do the same.

### Removing the aqualung
On the surface the instructor checks that you know how to purge the regulator by pressing the button on the second stage. This opens the valve and releases air, whether or not it is in your mouth. If you are sharing air underwater, or if you have your regulator knocked out, you need to be able to replace it without inhaling a mouthful of water.

On the bottom of the pool again, he indicates that you should watch him as he removes his regulator and holds it well away from his mouth. As he replaces it, he presses the purge button which releases a mass of bubbles. This stream of air blows all the water out of his mouth, and he can breathe normally again. Both you and your buddy repeat this exercise, and it seems remarkably straightforward in these controlled conditions.

Next you follow the same procedure, but first remove your aqualung and lay it on the bottom of the pool. You then take a

your mask, as it is bound to let in water at some time, perhaps simply because it has been knocked.

When on the surface mask clearing is most easily done by raising your head out of the water and lifting the mask away from the face so the water can drain out. When you are underwater you need a different technique.

Kneeling on the bottom again, the instructor points to each of you, then to his eyes — meaning 'You *watch* me'. He lets water into his mask and clears it. He then points to you to do the same. First

tip your head right back. Then with the fingers of one hand pressed on the top of the mask, breathe out through your nose. The additional air in the mask will try to escape around the edge which offers least resistance. As you are holding the top of the mask, it is the bottom that will be prized open slightly. As the water in your mask will have collected at the bottom, it will be forced out first, ahead of the air.

It will take you two or three goes at breathing out through your nose before the mask is properly cleared, but with practice that will

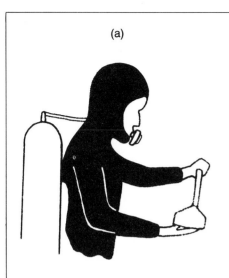

(a)

(b)

(c)

Putting on a mask underwater needs confidence and self-control and may take practice to perform calmly. (a) Hold the strap in one hand and the mask in the other.

(b) Place the mask over the eyes and pull the strap behind the head.

(c) Clear the water out of the mask by pressing your fingers along the top of the mask, tilting the head back and breathing out through your nose. The expelled air will force the water out of the bottom of the mask.

medium breath, turn the air off, remove your mouthpiece and place it carefully over the cylinder. An 'OK' signal to the instructor and you reverse the process. Air on, mouthpiece in, arms through the harness straps and cylinder safely on your back. Finally, you do up the waist buckle and give the 'OK' signal.

## Lesson Four

### Ditch and retrieve

By now you are becoming more confident about removing items of

The instructor demonstrates purging the regulator.

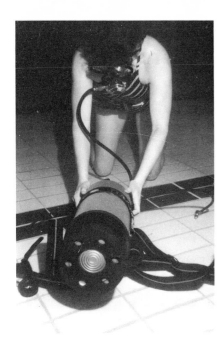

Placing the aqualung on the bottom of the pool helps build confidence in yourself and the equipment.

Replace the aqualung by slipping your hands through the harness straps and lifting the cylinder over your head.

your equipment and replacing them. The next exercise involves taking off your weight belt, aqualung, fins and mask, and leaving them all on the bottom while you surface. The last item you remove is the mouthpiece, so that you have air until the moment before you ascend. Then you turn off the air supply, look up to the surface, hold one arm above your head in case of obstacles, and breathe out as you go up. The object is then to dive down and replace everything with the minimum of fuss. The instructor remains on the bottom watching your progress.

Treading water on the surface, you look down and locate the weight belt — your first target. Without the weight, you would be too buoyant and would not be able to stay down. Then, with a medium size breath, you duck dive, grab the weight belt and drape it over one knee as you kneel on the other. It is rather tricky, but you must take your time and try to look as composed and controlled as possible.

Then, still holding your breath, you turn to the aqualung. You find the pillar valve, turn on the air, grasp the mouthpiece and put it in your mouth while pressing the purge button. Air! Although you could hold on a bit longer, it is still a relief when you can breathe normally again.

Next you position the weight belt around your waist and fasten the buckle. Then, locating the harness, you slip your arms through the shoulder straps and swing the cylinder onto your back.

Although you still cannot see very clearly, you *can* breathe and have no reason to panic. Reaching out with your arm, you pick up a dark object which looks about the size of a mask. Fortunately it is, and once you have swept the hair back away from your face, you place the mask over your eyes with one hand and slip the strap over your head with the other. Then it's fingers on the top of the mask, head back and a long steady breath out through your nose to clear the mask. With clear vision you can see your snorkel, which you slip under the mask strap, and your fins, which you put on easily. Looking at the instructor, you give the 'OK' signal which he returns.

Space is obviously limited in the pool, yet you need to learn the correct surfacing drill:

### Ascent procedure
○ Give each other the 'Ascend' signal.
○ Look up and fin gently towards the surface.
○ Keep together and keep an eye on each other.

○ Breathe normally; never hold your breath.
○ Rotate your body to give an all-round view.
○ Do not go up faster than your slowest, smallest bubbles — 15m per minute.
○ If a buoyancy aid has been partially inflated, vent it as you ascend.
○ Wind up the line on the surface marker buoy (often used in open-water dives).
○ Watch out for obstacles as you approach the surface.
○ Hold one arm above your head to protect it from unforeseen obstacles.
○ Once on the surface, check all round for possible approaching hazards.
○ Partially inflate your lifejacket.
○ Give the 'OK' signal to your buddy.
○ Exchange 'OK' signals with the boat or shore cover.
○ Replace the regulator with a snorkel if you are going to swim some distance on a calm surface, or wait until the boat comes to pick you up.

## Sharing air

If you keep a constant check on your contents gauge, and begin your ascent when the cylinder is about a quarter full, you should never run out of air underwater, unless some unforeseen hitch

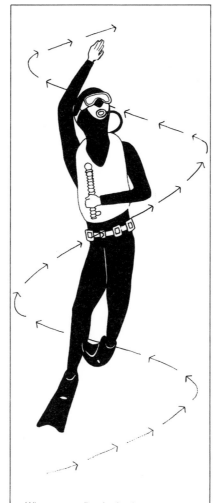

When ascending look where you are going and rotate to see all around. As you near the surface hold one arm above your head as protection against unexpected obstacles.

occurs. However, it is important to know how to share air with your buddy in case a regulator malfunctions, or one of you does run out of air because you have not been paying attention to the contents gauge.

Air sharing will *not* be possible if you do not keep an eye on each other, and stay within easy reach. It is essential that you practise correct buddy diving procedure at all times during a dive. If you do so there is much less chance of a minor incident turning into a major accident.

During training you are introduced to the air sharing technique under controlled conditions. The instructor demonstrates on land the position to adopt, with bodies half facing each other, and holding each other's harness straps (see diagram on p. 67). This ensures that you are close to each other and can both see clearly what is happening.

The diver giving air (the donor) is in control and takes the initiative. He always holds onto his regulator. He takes a breath, then removes the regulator second stage and directs it towards the victim's mouth. The victim helps guide it to his mouth, and, pressing the purge button, clears the mouthpiece. He takes two breaths — in, out, in, out — and

Sharing air or buddy breathing requires a calm, confident approach and a degree of co-ordination which is difficult to guarantee in a stressful situation. Half facing one another, the divers hold each other's harness strap. The donor holds the mouthpiece to the 'victim's' mouth and presses the purge button. The donor slowly breathes out so he is ready to take another lungful of air as soon as the 'victim' has taken two breaths.

lets go so the donor can take two breaths. Then the sequence is repeated.

While one diver is breathing through the regulator, the other should be breathing out slowly. This serves two purposes. The latter will be ready for a fresh breath of air as soon as the regulator comes back to him, without wasting time breathing out first. Secondly, and more importantly, it is good practice for when you rescue a diver from depth, and have to ascend while sharing air. As the air in your lungs expands when you surface, you must breathe out as you go up, or you will risk damaging your lungs.

In a real situation, if the victim is flustered or having difficulties, the donor, who is in control, may decide to take only one breath each time, and allow the victim more time with the regulator.

Once air sharing has been successfully achieved while kneeling down, you repeat the process with your buddy, but this time finning along the bottom of the pool. First you establish a breathing rhythm, then set off finning together whilst sharing your air supply. After finning about 25m you stop, switch to your buddy's air supply, then fin back to where you started.

When you are happy with

Air sharing or buddy breathing while finning along.

surface, you can go up at any time if you feel uneasy or unable to hold your breath longer than necessary.

## Assisted ascent

The next exercise is to share air while ascending. This is called an assisted ascent. It is the procedure you may need in a real diving situation, where one diver runs out of air, or his regulator develops a fault.

Maintaining the same basic air-sharing position, holding each other's harness straps, you establish a pattern of breathing with your buddy, then begin to surface. The donor keeps a look out for obstacles and rotates the two of you so that he can see all round. In the pool the water is too shallow to carry out this exercise properly. It is one of the procedures you will practise when you start diving in open water (see p. 96).

It is much simpler to carry out an assisted ascent using an octopus rig (see chapter 2), but the air-sharing technique must be learned because an octopus rig is not standard equipment.

## 'Blind' swim

As another confidence-builder, the training schedule includes a 'blind' swim, which simulates zero visibility. Wearing a blacked out

buddy breathing underwater, you might like to try this exercise which is useful as well as fun. A group of maybe six or eight people sit in a circle on the bottom of a swimming pool, with just one aqualung in the middle.

The mouthpiece is passed around the circle so each person takes two breaths, then passes it on. While waiting for the air to come round, you slowly exhale so that you are ready to take a breath when the regulator reaches you again. As you are in a swimming pool within easy reach of the mask, you are led by the hand around the bottom of the pool by the instructor. You have to trust him completely and relax in the faith that he will not let you crash into the side of the pool or another diver.

This exercise may be difficult for people with a strong streak of independence. But diving is a shared experience, not an independent one. Divers must work together.

After surfacing and confirming that all is well, you go down for another blind swim, but this time finding your own way along the tiled floor of the pool. The instructor fins along close by, but does not touch you. Seeing nothing but total blackness, you edge your way along the bottom, cautiously at first, but then more confidently.

### Alternate regulator and snorkel
At the surface again, you fin along breathing first through the regulator, then exchanging it for the snorkel. It is normal practice to use your snorkel on the surface. At the end of a dive, you would usually remove the regulator to conserve air, unless the surface is

choppy and water keeps entering your snorkel.

Next you tread water near the pool-side, while removing each item of gear in turn and passing it out. First your weight belt ... and immediately treading water becomes much easier, then your aqualung.

As both chlorine and salt water cause equipment to deteriorate, everything is thoroughly washed down with fresh water before being dismantled and put away.

## Lesson Five

### Using a lifejacket
Until now you have been training without a lifejacket. On an open water dive you should *always* wear a lifejacket. Chapter 2 described the different types of buoyancy aids available. Some are suitable for divers, others are not. The best buoyancy aid for a diver is the adjustable buoyancy lifejacket (ABLJ).

The instructor takes you through the different parts of an ABLJ, as illustrated in chapter 2. He gets you to inflate it orally by putting

While treading water pass each item of equipment out to an attendant at the side of the pool.

your mouth over the inflation hose, pressing the button and blowing. At the end of the blow you must release the button before taking your mouth away to breathe in, otherwise the valve would remain open and air from the jacket would escape or water would flow in. It takes about eight good breaths to fill the jacket.

Underwater, you will of course have to remove your mouthpiece each time before blowing into a jacket. This requires care and co-ordination, and is not recommended in stressful situations when an alternate air supply is available to supply the lifejacket.

Then you vent the jacket by pulling the toggle which opens the dump valve at the top of the jacket.

The second method of inflation uses the separate bottle of compressed air, stored at the bottom of the jacket. Before the dive, it is filled from the main cylinder. Making sure there is a good seal, the small cylinder is attached to the pillar valve before the regulator is fitted. The tap on the ABLJ bottle is opened, then the main air supply is turned on slightly. A hissing noise indicates that air is passing from the large to the small cylinder. The compression of air in the ABLJ cylinder produces heat, and feels

warm in your hand.

When full, the hissing stops. You turn off both taps but there is still a little air trapped between the two taps. Without venting this air you will not be able to separate the cylinders. Some cylinders have a button to press, which releases the air with a loud 'pop'; others have a tap which lets the air out more slowly.

Once you have taken the small cylinder off the main one, you screw it in place on the ABLJ. By turning the tap on the bottle, air is rapidly released into the lifejacket. You turn it off again before the jacket is absolutely full and the excess pressure valve is forced open.

This time you vent the ABLJ by pressing the button on the manual inflation hose and squeezing the air out of the jacket. When using this venting method underwater, the hose should be held above your head, as the air moves to the highest point in the jacket.

Some lifejackets are also linked to the main cylinder by a direct feed. This hose slots into a valve on the jacket. At the press of a button, air is fed directly from the main air supply into the jacket.

You do not try out the fourth method of inflation which some jackets have. This is the $CO_2$ cartridge, and can be used once only in an emergency on the

surface. It is operated by pulling a toggle.

### Controlling buoyancy

Now you are ready to try out buoyancy control on the bottom of the pool. The object of the exercise is to adjust your buoyancy using the lifejacket — first with the manual inflation hose, then using the bottle of compressed air and the dump valve.

You and your buddy get kitted up, helping each other where appropriate, and checking the operation of the weight belt, lifejacket, and so on.

You have purposely overweighted yourself a little to avoid surfacing as soon as you begin to inflate the jacket. On the bottom you take out your mouthpiece and blow into the inflation hose. You feel air going into the jacket, but your buoyancy does not change. Only when you replace the mouthpiece and fill your lungs again do you sense an increase in buoyancy. You repeat the process, blowing more air into the jacket. This time, when you take another lungful of air from the main cylinder, you begin to surface.

Next you hold the hose up, press the button and the air in the jacket is forced out, making you negatively buoyant again, so you

Inflating the ABLJ using the small cylinder of compressed air.

After suitable congratulations from the instructor, you then perform a similar operation using the compressed air from the ABLJ cylinder instead of the oral inflation hose. This method of inflation should be used sparingly, so there is always enough air in the small cylinder for emergency use when you will be less able to inflate the jacket orally.

On an open water dive you may need to swim some distance on the surface, perhaps to the shore or to the dive boat. This is much easier to do with an inflated lifejacket. You practise this in the pool, and soon appreciate that it is more relaxing finning along on your back, and stopping every now and then to check your direction.

## Lesson Six

### Basic rescue procedure

You need to know what to do if a diver gets into difficulty underwater, and you must be capable of acting quickly and sensibly. You have now covered many of the techniques which will be used in a rescue, and are building on skills you have already acquired.

The exact procedure adopted during an actual rescue will depend on the circumstances at the time. You should be

sink to the bottom.

Then you try again, this time a little less heavy-handedly. One breath has no effect, so you gradually add small amounts of air, until you feel your body begin to float up. Leaving your jacket alone, and with your regulator back in, you breathe out hard, emptying your lungs. That did the trick. Down you go again. You breathe in and go up, breathe out and go down. You have successfully achieved neutral buoyancy.

Venting the ABLJ by pressing the button on the hose.

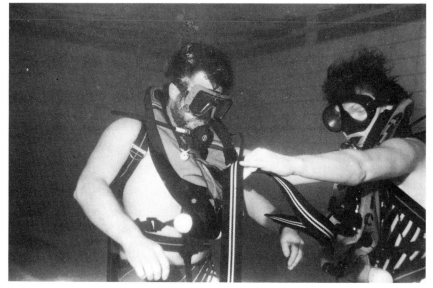

When rescuing an unconscious diver, grip his harness and remove his weight belt, dropping it well clear so it does not get tangled up in his gear.

sufficiently in control to assess the situation, plan what is best to do, and act quickly.

Learn the following procedure as a basic guideline for rescuing an unconscious diver from depth:
○ If the victim is trapped or tangled up, free him.
○ Take a firm grip of his harness. Remove his weight belt and dump it. During a rescue, never worry about losing items of gear; they can be replaced.
○ If you need more buoyancy to help you ascend, inflate his lifejacket using the small bottle or direct feed. If empty, inflate your own jacket. It is much

better *not* to drop your own belt or inflate your own jacket first, because this may mean you cannot get back down to the victim if he slips from your grasp.
○ If you are still not positively buoyant and have not started surfacing, begin finning.
○ Press your clenched hand into the victim's diaphragm to encourage him to breathe out during the ascent — to avoid a burst lung.

○ Note your rate of ascent. If it is too fast, stop finning and vent your lifejacket. Your ascent rate should not exceed 15m (about 50ft) per minute. As a rule of thumb, do not go up faster than your slowest, smallest bubbles.
○ As you near the surface, look out for obstacles and hold one hand above your head if necessary.
○ On the surface the lifejacket may be fully inflated because the air in it will have expanded as you surfaced. If so you will need to let some air out until it is about three-quarters full. If it

72

Still holding the harness, lift him by pushing a clenched fist into his diaphragm.

was not inflated underwater, do so now.
○ Clear the airway by removing the mouthpiece and mask.
○ Apply mouth-to-nose resuscitation. You use the mouth-to-nose method, rather than mouth-to-mouth, when in

Apply mouth-to-nose resuscitation while in the water. Tilt the head right back to open the airway but hold the mouth closed. During training blow beyond the person's face.

the water because it is difficult to check that the airway via the mouth is clear.

When training, resuscitation should be *simulated*, as it is dangerous to breathe into the lungs of a conscious person. This is done by supporting the person's head and tilting it right back to open the windpipe (see photograph). Then, with the other hand, hold the person's chin so that his mouth is closed. By finning, raise yourself above the

On the surface remove his mouthpiece and mask.

victim at the same time as tilting the body towards you. This brings his nose very close to your mouth. In an emergency you would seal the nose with your mouth and blow air into the lungs. During training you would normally blow beyond the person's face, but your instructor may ask you to make a proper seal to show that you can do it effectively.

After the breath, relax back into the water and prepare for the next breath. You should give four quick breaths to fill his lungs, then settle down to a rhythm of 12-15 breaths per minute, or one every four or five seconds.

○ Continue giving mouth-to-nose resuscitation while summoning help, with the waving clenched fist signal (see pp. 56-7).

## Lesson Seven

### Full diving equipment

You have accomplished most of the *exercises* which make up the training course, but these have been done in ideal conditions. You are now ready to progress to situations which are closer to a realistic open water dive.

When you put on a full wet suit, several things change. Not only does it take longer to get ready for a dive, but your movements when wearing the suit are

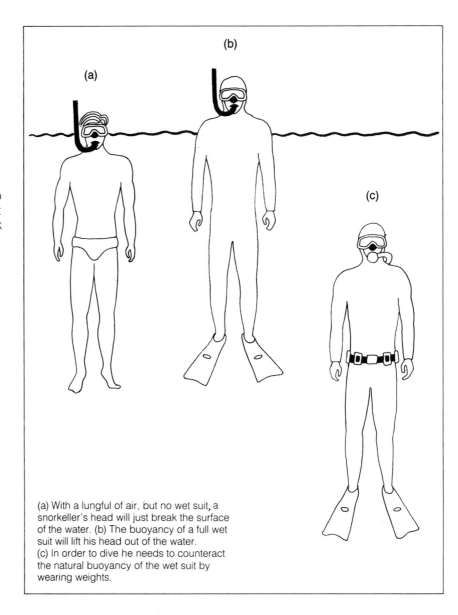

(a) With a lungful of air, but no wet suit, a snorkeller's head will just break the surface of the water. (b) The buoyancy of a full wet suit will lift his head out of the water.
(c) In order to dive he needs to counteract the natural buoyancy of the wet suit by wearing weights.

restricted. Buoyancy, too, is dramatically different. The tiny bubbles of gas in the suit make it positively buoyant. As a result you need more weights to make you neutrally buoyant in the water. A fully kitted up diver may wear 6-10kg of weight, as opposed to 0-2kg without a suit.

With wet suits on, you and your buddy put on your lifejackets, aqualungs and weight belts, and check that everything is in order. A buddy check ensures that both air cylinders are turned on, the buckles of the weight belts and harnesses are accessible and operable, and the lifejackets can be inflated by either member of the buddy pair.

By this stage you are very hot and longing to get into the water. You put the wet suit hood up, trying to tuck your hair out of the way. After cleaning your mask, you find it awkward to put it on with the hood framing your face. But you manage to wedge it in place, and are happy with the seal. Fins on and then your gloves. Like your wet suit, these are made of neoprene, and you are surprised at how clumsy they feel. When you are all set, you and your buddy follow the instructor into the water.

To show that your wet suit has not deprived you of all your mobility, you each complete a forward and a backward roll.

Then, after a quick demonstration by the instructor, you each flood your masks in turn, and clear them. Manipulation is more awkward wearing gloves, but you soon become accustomed to it.

Next you remove the mouthpiece and hold it away from your face before replacing it. Kneeling on the bottom, you begin sharing air with your buddy, as you did earlier in the training. Once you have established a steady rhythm, you fin the length of the pool, change places and fin back again. While continuing to share air, you fin towards the surface, rotating, with your arm above your head, and looking up.

Finally, you remove your weight belt and aqualung while treading water, and hand them to a helper on the pool-side.

## Lesson Eight

### A rescue in full kit

Once you are fully kitted up and kneeling on the bottom of the pool, the instructor watches as you each remove and replace your weight belt, fins, mask, cylinder and regulator.

Next you simulate a rescue underwater. Your buddy pretends to be unconscious on the bottom of the pool. From 10m away you fin rapidly towards him, grab his harness strap and jettison his weight belt. Then, positioning yourself under him and pressing his diaphragm, you bring him to the surface.

After inflating his lifejacket using the small cylinder, you remove his mouthpiece and mask, hold his head back, supporting his neck, and start simulated mouth-to-nose resuscitation. To show that you can keep this up for a while, you need to carry on for three minutes, which seems like an eternity. After the initial four breaths you wave a clenched fist to the instructor by way of summoning help.

### Summary of pool training
○ Fitness/swimming test.
○ Medical examination, including a chest X-ray.
○ Prevent mask from misting up.
○ Clear the snorkel tube on surfacing.
○ Introduction to the cylinder, regulator, contents gauge, and weight belt.
○ Hand signals.
○ Correct any faults immediately.
○ Breathe through your mouth, not your nose.
○ Retrieve mask, fins and snorkel, and replace them on the surface.
○ Always dive with a buddy.

A swimming pool provides a sheltered, controlled environment suitable for the early stages of diver training.

○ Adopt good buddy procedure.
○ Assemble the aqualung.
○ Different modes of entering the water.
○ Testing buoyancy.
○ Forward and backward rolls.
○ Mask clearing.
○ Removing and replacing equipment underwater.
○ How to ascend.

○ How to share air with your buddy.
○ Always wear a suitable lifejacket while diving, and be well-practised in its use.
○ Rescue procedure.

At this point in your training you are ready to go diving only if accompanied by a diver who is qualified to supervise novices. In chapter 5 you will see what a typical first open water dive might entail. Then chapter 6 will take you to the stage where you can dive with a buddy, without being under supervision.

# 5. First open-water dive

You have reached the stage in your pool training when you can remove your mask, replace and clear it; you are happy to share air with your buddy; and you can simulate a pretty convincing rescue. You feel confident and relaxed in the water.

Now it's time for the real thing — time for your first open-water dive. This might be from the shore or from a boat. This chapter looks at what you might experience on your first dive from an inflatable boat.

The main thing you will discover is that it is quite different from the comfortable and predictable environment of the swimming pool. For a start, getting into and out of the water is more of an effort than jumping off the side of the pool. The surface of the water will almost certainly be choppy and the waves will buffet you around. And if you are diving in a cool climate, the water can be punishingly cold.

Your instructor should go through exactly what you are going to do so that nothing comes as an unpleasant shock, although cold water will be a shock, however much you are warned of it.

### Several days before the dive
Your first dive actually begins long before you get in the water. Preparations start with assembling all your gear, and checking it. As you are fairly new to diving, the

Open-water diving is seldom as straightforward as diving in a pool. The surface may be choppy; there may be currents; the visibility may be poor; it will probably be colder; there are likely to be more unpredictable obstacles; and it can be much deeper.

chances are that you will be borrowing or hiring at least some of the equipment. Several days before the dive, make sure that each item will be available for your use on the day.

Carry out a series of checks to reduce the likelihood of a last minute panic and to help put you in the right frame of mind for the dive. You are thinking about the equipment; you are thinking about the dive; and you are imagining how you would deal with different situations. This mental tuning up is all part of diving, and will help give you confidence and peace of mind.

## Checks
○ Check the condition of all the equipment you are likely to use (see chapter 2).
○ Check that all new gear fits you properly and is adjusted correctly.
○ Check that your lifejacket functions correctly and that you are familiar with each method of inflation and venting. Do not assume it will be like the one you borrowed during pool training, or that it will be like the instructor's deluxe model. If your lifejacket is fitted with a $CO_2$ canister, this is for use only

Cylinders being filled with compressed air.

in an emergency and is not re-usable, so obviously cannot be tested before the dive.
○ Check the cylinder is in test.
○ Check the cylinder is fully charged. It may be your responsibility to get the cylinder filled with compressed air. This can be done at most dive shops and dive centres. Some clubs also have their own compressor.
○ Go through the checklist of equipment at the end of chapter 2 and include all the items relevant to your dive.

When you have gathered all the gear together and are happy with it, decide how you are going to get to the dive site. Are you sure about where and when you are meeting the others?

Don't go on a heavy drinking session the previous evening. A hangover is the last thing you want on a dive, and being sick underwater is more than most people can cope with. If you find yourself in this state, the technique is to remove the regulator while you are being sick, then purge and replace it immediately, so you can catch your breath. If you cough or sneeze underwater, you should be able to keep your mouthpiece in, and so avoid taking in water when you gasp for breath.

**What *really* happens?**
Let's follow the likely course of

events on a typical first dive with a club.

When you arrive at the appointed location, it is drizzling slightly and there is nobody else in sight. Trying to suppress your worries, you check you have come to the right place at the right time. You're a few minutes early and so you scout around the area.

A sandy cove, flanked by high cliffs, drops vertically down to scattered boulders where the waves are breaking. You try not to imagine what would happen if you were diving too close to the rocks.

The instructor's car swings into the car park, towing a trailer carrying the club's inflatable boat. A surge of adrenalin hits you as you realise your first dive looks like becoming a reality.

Although you are not in charge of the dive, you should understand what the dive organiser's job entails. Listen to what he says and be a willing helper when there's work to be done.

## The dive plan and briefing

What is the aim of the dive? In the case of your first open-water dive, this will simply be to introduce you to the new environment, and to help you be confident and competent within it.

The instructor will be your buddy

on this occasion. Your first dive will be in shallow water — perhaps 8m or 9m — and you will always be within easy reach of the surface. Yet many of the principles you learned during training still apply. You will need to clear your ears on descent, and breathe out while ascending slowly, to avoid a burst lung.

During the briefing, your instructor explains exactly what he has planned for the dive and refreshes your memory on a few points: 'Show me what you would do if you hit your mask and let in some water?' In reply you slide your mask over your head, and demonstrate mask-clearing by tilting your head back and pressing on the top of the mask with the tips of your fingers, at the same time breathing out through your nose.

He then goes through clearing ears, adjusting buoyancy and sharing air. You have done this many times during training, but it is far from boring. The excitement of your first dive and the knowledge that your life may depend on getting it right give you a strong vested interest.

Without these preparations you may forget something crucial to the dive, and will probably feel tense and accident-prone. Careful, methodical preparation is important for all divers, not only for the novice diver who is understandably apprehensive. Just as no sane pilot will take off without a full pre-flight check, divers must adopt similar stringent diving procedures.

It is your instructor's job to help you approach the dive with confidence, but if at any time you feel over-anxious about the situation, do not soldier on ignoring your worries. You can decide to call off the dive at any time, even after you have entered the water. Better that than be put off diving because you are having an off day.

While the dive leader assesses the conditions — the weather, size of waves and so on — you gather your gear together and start kitting up.

You notice that one or two of the more experienced divers have put on a pair of tights before getting into their wet suits ... and not just the ladies! When you try to pull on your wet suit over your clammy feet, you realise why. Besides keeping you warmer, nylon tights make it much easier to put on a closely fitting wet suit, especially when damp. Rubbing talcum powder over your arms and legs also reduces the friction between your skin and the neoprene.

Just as you finish struggling with your long johns, the instructor calls

Hold the contents gauge away from you as you turn on the air.

for help with the boat. The trailer carrying the boat is uncoupled from his car and ten of you guide it down the beach. At the water's edge it is swung round and backed into the water. With someone steadying the head of the trailer, the rest of the team lifts the boat onto the shallow surf and then turns the boat so the bow is pointing into the waves.

One diver waits with the boat while the rest fetch the gear. Looking at your great heap of equipment you decide to make two journeys down the beach. But just then the instructor stops you and says, 'It's only a short boat ride to the dive site, and you'll be one of the first to go in the water. You may as well get fully kitted up now and walk down to the boat with everything on. It'll be much easier than trying to put it on in the boat while it's tossing around on the waves.'

## Kitting up

With the cylinder upright, you fit your regulator and air contents gauge onto the pillar valve, having first checked the 'O' ring is in place and free from bits of dirt. Holding the gauge away from your face

Check the contents gauge to make sure there is plenty of air in the cylinder for the dive you have planned.

and turning the tap on top of the cylinder, you hear a hiss as a sudden rush of air fills the rubber hoses. Then it's quiet. No leaks.

You check the reading on the gauge — 200 bar (just under 3,000 psi), perfect for this cylinder, a 2,000-litre aluminium cylinder.

Next you turn off the air supply and purge the hoses to release the pressure so that you can take the regulator off again. Carefully repeating the procedure in your mind, you take the small cylinder from your lifejacket and screw it onto the pillar valve of the main cylinder. You open the tap on the small cylinder, then turn on the main supply very slowly. Air hisses into the small cylinder and the bottle feels warm as the air compresses. You close the small tap, then the main tap, and press the button which releases the air between the two. After unscrewing the small cylinder, you replace it in your lifejacket, which you partially inflate to make sure everything is working as it should. Finally, you put the regulator back on the main cylinder.

Despite the chill wind, you've left your wet suit jacket off until now because the sleeves of the jacket restrict your arm movements, making it more awkward to get your things together. You leave the hood off for now, as it makes hearing difficult.

82

The lifejacket should go on before the aqualung or weight belt, as it is the last item to be removed at the end of the dive.

After your wet suit jacket you turn to your lifejacket. This goes on before the aqualung and weight belt because it should be the last item to be taken off at the end of

the dive (except the wet suit) in case, at any time, you need to use it to give you buoyancy.

Next come all the bits and pieces — watch, depth gauge, knife and compass. Then the instructor lifts up your aqualung, helps you put it on and reminds you to clip the direct feed into your lifejacket. The weight belt is the last item to be fitted because it is the first to be ditched.

### Weights for correct buoyancy

Salt water is denser than fresh water so you are more buoyant in the sea than in an inland lake or in a swimming pool. As a result you need more weight to keep you down in the sea. Also, the more neoprene you are wearing, the more buoyant you will be, and the more weight you need to wear.

Also, because different people's bodies have different densities, each requires a different amount of weight. So you need to know what is appropriate for *you* in salt and fresh water, and when wearing different amounts of neoprene.

Bearing in mind the amount of neoprene you are wearing, and the fact that this dive is in salt water, your instructor recommends to put on 8kg of lead.

Now you are ready. It is easier to carry the gear when you are wearing it, but you still find it takes quite an effort to stagger down the beach wearing everything, and carrying only your mask, fins, snorkel and gloves in your dive bag.

## On the surface

One of the experienced divers is in charge of the boat and tells you

Always carry out a buddy check to make sure everything is in order and that you know how to release his weight belt and operate his lifejacket.

when to get in. When everyone is in position the boat sets out over the breakers. The throttle is opened up and you roar out across the waves. You hold on to one of the boat handles to steady yourself, and throw your head back to feel the wind and spray on your face.

The skipper lines the boat up with a couple of markers on the shore, then stops the boat and lets down a line to measure the depth. Just over 8m, perfect.

The anchor is dropped over the side and someone's T-shirt is taken with it, as the line quickly unravels. You make a mental note: make sure that no gear is tangled up in the line *before* throwing the anchor overboard.

Your heart starts beating faster

as the big moment approaches. You look up at your instructor and he nods. It is time for the buddy check.

### Buddy check

Because of the wide variety of equipment designs, and the possibility of making a mistake while gearing up, it is important to carry out a proper buddy check before each dive. Your buddy checks your gear is OK. You check his gear is OK, and confirm that you know how to work it. It is essential for each of you to know exactly how to inflate the other person's lifejacket and how to release the weights and cylinder.

You go through all the various hand signals. Besides refreshing your memory, this serves as an additional confidence-builder. 'Be bold about giving signals,' says your instructor firmly. 'Let your buddy know how you are feeling, where you want to go, and so on. And at the same time, pay attention to his needs. If we get separated, look all around for me. If I'm not there, return to the surface *slowly*. But don't worry, I'll be there!'

Your whole body is tingling with anticipation as your instructor repeats the dive plan: 'We will be the first pair to enter the water. I'll enter the water first from this side, then you roll backwards off your side of the boat, holding onto the safety line. When you surface give the OK signal to the skipper of the boat, then swim around to the anchor line. We'll go down the anchor line together. Remember to clear your ears as you go. We'll stop on the bottom at 8m and check everything is OK — buoyancy, ears and so on. Then, as long as you're happy, we'll fin gently along the bottom against the current for ten minutes, turn round and come back. The visibility is not too good today, so we shall have to keep close together. Take your time, we're not kamikaze lemmings. OK?' Yes.

You lean forwards to put on your fins, and the aqualung on your back feels heavy and unwieldy. Next you slip the hood onto your head. You feel quite warm now in your thick wet suit, and trickles of

perspiration are beginning to run down your face.

Next the mask; you spit on the inside, rub it in with your fingers and then rinse it off in the sea. When your mask is in position, someone checks that your air is turned on. You ask if it is all clear behind, then put the regulator in your mouth. Holding your mask to your face with your right hand and cylinder with your left, you roll back into the water holding onto the safety line so as not to drift away or plunge to the bottom.

## Taking the plunge

At first you feel nothing as the churning white foam engulfs you. Then, as you start to straighten out and come to the surface, threads of cold water find their way into your wet suit. Still submerged, you gasp for breath, thankful that the regulator is still securely in your mouth.

You bob up and look up at those in the boat. They suddenly look very warm and snug in contrast to your newly-chilled state. One of them is giving you the OK signal. You return it clearly and deliberately, then turn to make your way to the anchor line at the bow. Your buddy is already there. He gives you another OK signal which you return. Then he gives the thumbs down signal for descent.

Recalling your pool training, you float on the surface looking down. You bend your body at the waist, flip your fins into the air and begin to dive. After a few quick kicks, you realise you are still at the surface and are not descending as you should. Why? Not enough weight, you are too buoyant.

You pull yourself towards the boat using the anchor line and call out for another weight. 'Hand your weight belt in,' says someone on the boat, and he adds another 2kg of lead. Then, careful not to drop it, you refit the weight belt and are all set to try again.

You are no longer quite so cold; the layer of water caught between you and your wet suit has now warmed up and is providing good insulation.

### Going down
This time a few strong kicks do the trick and you look back at the receding surface and the bottom of the boat. Although it was choppy on the surface, it is much calmer now, and you relax a little. Following the anchor line, you begin to fin gently down.

Almost immediately, a dull ache on your eardrums reminds you to equalise the pressure. Swallow. That helped a bit. Swallow again. Not much difference. You stop, grasp the anchor line with your left hand and pull yourself up about a metre. Your legs drift down until you are suspended in an upright position. Squeezing your nose with thumb and index finger of your right hand, and not letting air escape through your mouth, you blow firmly until your tubes are clear again.

Your buddy is alongside and you exchange the OK signal again. It seems like a lot of OKs, but that is reassuring, and much better than too few.

You continue to descend and find that clearing your ears seems to get easier. Drifting down takes very little effort; your body feels weightless, a marked contrast to the clumsy figure lumbering down the beach half an hour earlier. You become aware that the only sound you can hear is the low grumble of your expelled air, followed by the hiss of your inward breath.

## On the bottom

Unexpectedly, the sea-bed comes into view. It is a dark grey scene strewn with small rocks, patches of sea-grass and algae. You see the anchor neatly wedged in a cleft. At the bottom you let your feet sink down until you are kneeling by the anchor, facing your buddy.

You are slightly negatively buoyant, so you look down for the direct feed button. Just two short squirts of air are enough to give the buoyancy you need. Then,

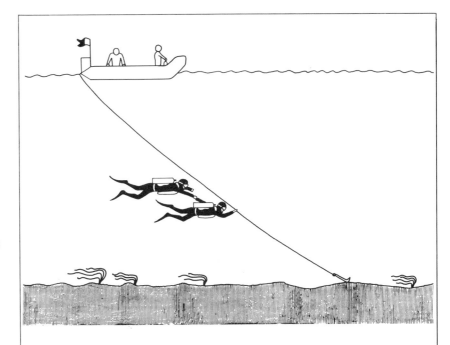

Begin a dive by swimming into the current so that during the second half of the dive, when you are tired and have a depleted air supply, you will be able to return to the anchor without struggling against the current.

recalling the buoyancy tests you did in the pool, you breathe in deeply and hold your breath for a couple of seconds. After a slight delay, your body floats up. Then you breathe out, emptying your lungs, and sink to the bottom. Of course you knew it would work like that, but it is still fun to prove it... and in the sea, too.

Your buddy gives a firm OK signal. 'OK' you reply. Then he points to his ears and gives the OK again. OK you reply, ears are fine.

Visibility is about 3m; you can see the ends of your fins, but not very much further. 'Easy to get lost' you think. Your buddy holds out his

hand and you grasp it, suddenly feeling secure again. With his other hand he points to indicate the direction to go. You both push off from the bottom and head into the gentle current.

You fin along about a metre from the sea-bed. It feels like flying. Although it is dark and murky, you are entranced by the fact you are gliding almost effortlessly over the rocks and sea-grasses. It's hard to believe how easy it is.

Just ahead of you a couple of dark fish shapes are startled and flash off out of sight. Your buddy squeezes and shakes your hand, then points with his other hand. At

first you cannot make out what he means; you stop and stare, but don't see anything. You sink down, pushing your face towards the spot. Suddenly a little crab scurries off and you jerk your head up again. Continuing along the bottom you notice three more crabs, a starfish and several fish you cannot identify.

Your buddy looks at you from time to time, checking everything is all right. You feel confident and give him the OK signal, which he returns. He points to his own contents gauge and then to yours. It reads 100 bar, while his reads 120 bar. You feel your heart rate increasing, 'I'm breathing too heavily; I'll run out of air! Then you calm down, remembering that different people use different quantities of air. It is quite normal for less experienced divers to use up their supply more quickly. They are more apprehensive, and expend more energy than is really necessary.

Looking at his watch, your buddy gives the stop signal, then indicates it's time to return the way you have come. On the way back you become more aware of your body. The floating sensation feels magical. You give a shiver, as you

OK signal from boat to water.

All sorts of interesting creatures may be hiding in the nooks and crannies.

notice again how cold the water is. Your cheeks and lips are almost numb, and you wiggle your toes to make sure they are still intact.

## Coming up

Back at the anchor again, you both stop and exchange the OK signal. Your contents gauge registers 50 bar. Plenty of time to surface; well within limits. Your buddy gives the 'thumbs up' and you begin to

surface. Finning very gently, you drift upwards, sliding the anchor rope through one hand.

Mentally you check off the correct procedure: ascend slowly — no faster than your slowest bubbles. Breathe normally. Release some air from your lifejacket as your buoyancy increases. Look all around you to make sure there is no danger. Look to the surface — the outline of the boat can be seen against the sky.

## Back on the surface

As you approach the surface, you are still rising even when you stop finning. Careful to avoid the boat, you break the surface in an explosion of noise. Suddenly your breath is much noisier and you can hear the waves slapping against the side of the boat. Your buddy is there, giving the 'OK'. You return it.

People on the boat are saying something, but you cannot make out what it is. Someone is leaning over giving the OK signal.' Yes, yes, I'm fine.' You signal OK as your face disappears below the surface once more. When you bob up again the person on the boat says something to you. Your reply comes out as a muffled moan and you realise your regulator is still in your mouth. Taking it out, you splutter 'What?', then get a mouthful of water as a wave washes over you. Finning harder to keep your face out of the water, you purge then replace your regulator.

'Inflate your jacket,' says a voice. You fumble for the button and give it a very positive push. Suddenly

Getting out of the water is much easier after you have handed the weight belt and aqualung to an attendant on the boat.

life is much easier, as your weight is supported by a cushion of air.

'Hand me your weight belt,' says the voice again. Weight belt? Right. You reach round your waist for the clasp. You find and undo it. Wrong, that was the waist strap of your cylinder! Finally you locate the weight belt clamp, which has slipped round to the side.

Careful not to drop it, you release the clamp and hold it out for the person in the boat to take. As soon

as you are rid of the weights it is all much easier.

Next, your aqualung. You unclip the direct feed line. Then, with the waist strap already undone, you slip one arm out of the harness. It is more awkward than you thought; you are beginning to feel tired and your wet suit restricts movement. The helper in the boat grabs the harness and you swing round to release your other arm. Just in time you remember the regulator and spit it out as it is lifted onto the boat.

Keeping your mask on, you hold onto the side of the boat with both hands and fin hard. This projects you out of the water and you land half over the side of the boat. Now it is a simple matter to pivot around, placing first one leg then the other on the side. One kind person slips your fins off and you are free to sit upright and catch your breath again. To release the pressure on your chest you unzip your jacket.

### Look after your gear
While you are telling everyone how wonderful it was, you gather your fins and weight belt and stuff them into your dive bag, together with your mask and snorkel. Although the sun is out, you can feel the breeze through your wet suit, so you grab your windproof anorak and pull it on.

Next it's gloves off, followed by watch, depth gauge and knife. You turn off the air on your cylinder and purge the regulator ready to take it off back on the beach. The aqualung is then laid flat alongside your buddy's.

Later you will rinse out all the gear in fresh water, but now all you can do is to keep it together and out of other people's way as the next batch prepare to dive. While two more pairs of divers go down, you munch on a biscuit and your buddy/instructor talks through the dive with you.

When you are back on dry land, it's time to fill in your logbook while you remember the details. Make a note of the maximum depth, time, equipment used, weights needed, visibility and the marine life you saw.

For the rest of the day you have a permanent grin on your face. You feel physically invigorated and mentally stimulated. Your first dive and you are still in one piece!

Besides wanting to tell everyone how exciting diving is, you are already looking forward to your second open-water dive.

### Dos and don'ts
*Do*
- check your gear several days before a dive
- prepare yourself mentally as well as physically
- make sure you know the arrangements for meeting before the dive
- plan your dive, and understand the aim of the dive
- conduct a thorough buddy check
- act slowly and methodically
- help others to kit up, or to lift their gear back onto the boat
- keep in constant contact with your buddy underwater
- breathe regularly and calmly
- keep checking air contents gauge, depth gauge and watch
- breathe normally when ascending
- watch out for obstacles, such as the boat, while ascending
- keep the gear in the boat tidy
- rinse out all equipment in fresh water
- make a copy of the checklist on page 40 and store it with your dive gear so you can easily identify those items which you need for a particular dive (*note:* you won't necessarily want to take the torch, for example, unless you plan to go on a night dive).

*Don't*
- drink and dive
- dive if you feel nervous or unhappy
- continue descending if you cannot clear your ears
- ascend faster than your slowest bubbles
- hold your breath during the ascent
- forget to have your qualifying dives signed up in your logbook

Pass the aqualung into the boat at the end
of a dive to make it easier to climb on board.

Stow your gear in a dive bag to keep it
together and out of other people's way.

# 6. Completing basic training

Training is no longer restricted to sheltered waters. You have started diving in the sea and found that, although cold, it is tremendously exciting.

You are now familiar with all the essential scuba gear and how to use it. You understand the importance of certain physical laws, and their effects on divers. You can carry out basic tasks, such as mask clearing and air sharing. And you are beginning to come to terms with the rescue procedure.

Your first few open-water dives provide the opportunity to start applying the skills you have learned so far. At the same time, there are new techniques to be mastered and more experience to be gained.

Again, sessions on theory run concurrently with the practical exercises. More advanced rescue skills, covered in a lecture, are put into practice first in the pool and then in open water. A talk on underwater navigation is followed by a dive in which you use a compass to help you decide your course underwater. And an explanation of the use of a surface marker buoy (SMB) is followed by a dive in which you use an SMB.

A good training course builds up your experience in a logical progression. This enables you to take each step in your stride, confidently and eagerly.

By the end of this chapter you will have covered all you need to know to dive safely with a buddy of your standard or higher. A signature on the right piece of paper will enable you to hire equipment and have cylinders refilled at dive centres throughout the world.

## Different diving conditions

Besides practising a series of rescue procedures and navigation exercises, the course requires you to carry out at least ten qualifying dives in a variety of conditions. These may include:
- ○ a shore dive
- ○ a dive in sea water
- ○ a dive in fresh water
- ○ a dive from a boat
- ○ a dive in poor visibility (less than 2m)
- ○ a dive in a slow-moving current (about 1 knot)
- ○ a dive in water colder than 10°C (50°F)
- ○ a dive to 25m (82ft)

An ideal sequence of training might go something like this:

## Rescue procedure in the pool

Diving is a joint activity, not only because it is more enjoyable to share the experience, but it is also

safer. Your buddy's life may depend on your ability to think clearly and act quickly. At the same time, your life is in his hands if something unexpected happens.

Because of the risks involved, rescue procedures play a dominant role in the training course. Once you can handle your own equipment — first in the pool, then in open water — the emphasis shifts to rescue techniques. These should be covered in theory and in the pool *before* your first open-water dive. It is quite conceivable that the instructor may need *your* help during a dive, and you must be prepared for it right from dive number 1.

In the pool you repeat rescue exercises, first without a wet suit, then with one. You bring up your buddy, who is simulating unconsciousness, by jettisoning his weight belt, gripping his harness strap and lifting him to the surface. You take off his mouthpiece and mask to help his breathing, and pretend to give him four quick breaths to simulate resuscitation.

In a real situation you would, of course, establish first that he had stopped breathing. His skin would appear blue-grey and his chest would not be moving (difficult to see on a fully-kitted diver).

Although there are several methods of artifical respiration, the mouth-to-nose method is the only one which should be applied while treading water.

Once you have filled his lungs, you inflate his lifejacket to about three-quarters full, then summon help by giving the 'Distress' signal (see pp. 72ff for complete sequence of controlled lift).

## Towing

On this occasion, you act as if help is not at hand, and begin towing the diver using the *extended arm tow*. This method gives you plenty of room to fin freely and allows you to swim on your back or on your side.

With your arm fully extended hold the victim under the chin with your hand in a pistol grip position. This will extend his airway, and you can quickly adopt the position for resuscitation by bringing your cupped hand towards you. While you are towing, pause every 20 seconds to apply four mouth-to-nose breaths, then continue towing.

Now you have to land the 'unconscious' person while maintaining mouth-to-nose resuscitation. Careful to protect the head as much as possible, slip your arms under each of his arms. Next place his hands one on top of the other on the pool-side, and hold them with one of your hands. Making sure you do not let go of his hands, get out of the pool, and

92

From the extended arm tow it is easy to pull the body towards you ready for mouth-to-nose resuscitation.

Grip both his wrists with one hand, then lift yourself out.

grab his wrists. Bending your knees, not your back, haul him out of the pool and *gently* lay him down in the coma position (see

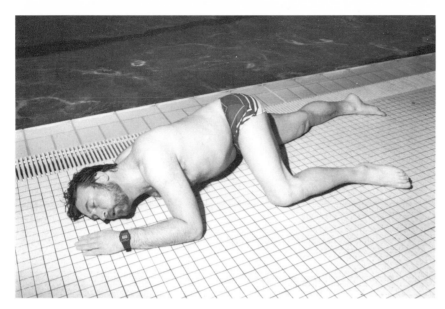

The coma position supports the body in such a way that the chest is not restricted and the head is well back.

one just above the base of the sternum (see photograph below left). Keeping your arms straight, press down sharply and release six times in quick succession (about one a second). During training do not actually apply pressure.

Next, start mouth-to-mouth resuscitation, with his head well back. Then try to find the pulse on his neck (the carotid artery). If there is no response apply six more compressions of cardiac massage. Continue this sequence of massage and resuscitation (six to

photograph above). Then send for medical help.

### Cardiac massage
If the diver's heart has stopped, apply cardiac massage, first making sure that his airway is not blocked by his tongue, vomit or seaweed. With the patient lying face up, put both hands together and place the heel of the bottom

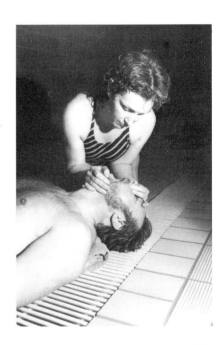

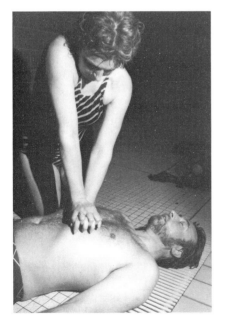

◄ Cardiac massage is simulated during training. With both hands together and the heel of the bottom hand just above the base of the sternum (breastbone), press down enough to push the sternum down about 4 - 5 cm (for an average adult).

Mouth-to-mouth resuscitation: with the victim's head well back, pinch the nose with one hand and hold the mouth open with the other.

Build up your experience by diving under different conditions and entering water in different ways: from a boat, sandy beach or rocky cove.

one) until you detect a pulse. Then continue resuscitation until he starts to breathe, or medical help arrives. Once he is breathing put him in the coma position.

Even if someone appears to be dead, you should continue to try to revive him. The body's responses may have slowed down because of the cold, and you may not be able

to detect breathing or a pulse, yet he may be alive.

The entire rescue exercise is strenuous and should if possible be carried out by two people. You will find ordinary dives a relaxing pleasure by contrast.

### First dive
A shallow dive, no more than 10m, introduces you to the open-water environment (see chapter 5). The conditions are calm and the instructor, who is also your buddy,

is careful to ensure that everything runs smoothly. Apart from the essentials of buoyancy control and ear clearing as you go down, there are no specific tasks to perform on this dive. The idea of the exercise is to help you enjoy the experience of diving, so that you are inspired to forge ahead with enthusiasm.

### Building up experience
On subsequent dives you progressively add to your experience by entering and leaving

the water in a variety of ways — along a gently sloping beach, over a rocky beach, from a jetty, from a pier, via steps and from different types of boat.

After each dive you fill in your logbook, noting the date and location, equipment used, aim of the dive, bottom time, maximum depth, observations made, tasks achieved and the section of the training for which the dive qualifies you. Get this signed by your instructor and you will not only have an essential record of qualifying dives, but also a

As a part of the buddy check go through the hand signals.

satisfying reminder of the dives you have been on.

When walking anywhere wearing full kit, you are top-heavy and unstable. Look out for rough or slippery ground, and avoid battling through surf.

During the second dive, again in calm conditions, you begin by finning along the surface for about 50m, using the snorkel. At 12m on the sandy sea-bed you practise exercises which have become almost second nature to you in the swimming pool: adjusting buoyancy, flooding your mask, then clearing it; removing the mouthpiece, then replacing it; sharing air with the instructor. You

Jumping in off the side of a jetty.

also begin to make a habit of checking your watch, depth gauge and contents gauge at frequent intervals. When your cylinder is a quarter full, you and your buddy ascend together.

## Buddy diving

Sport divers dive in pairs and each diver is responsible for the safety of the other. On every dive you must observe correct buddy diving procedure:
○ always try to act in an atmosphere of mutual co-operation
○ decide which of you will be the lead diver on each dive
○ discuss the planned dive beforehand
○ help your buddy put on his gear
○ check buckles, lifejacket inflation and air pressure

- descend together
- constantly check that your buddy is OK
- communicate with him using hand signals
- ascend together
- discuss the dive and the points arising from it
- be the buddy you would like to dive with

If you become separated from your buddy, stop and look around for him. If you do not see him within 15 or 20 seconds, return to the surface. As long as he is not in trouble and is observing the correct procedure, you will meet him there and can continue the dive together. If he does not appear, you should be able to find his bubbles and follow these down.

### Rescue in open water

Again repeating what has already been covered in the pool, you share air with your buddy as you return to the surface (assisted ascent), remembering to breathe out when your buddy has the regulator.

On the next dive your buddy simulates unconsciousness at 5m, and you lift him to the surface by holding his harness strap, jettisoning his weight belt and finning gently upwards. As you near the surface you watch for obstacles. On the surface you remove his mouthpiece and mask,

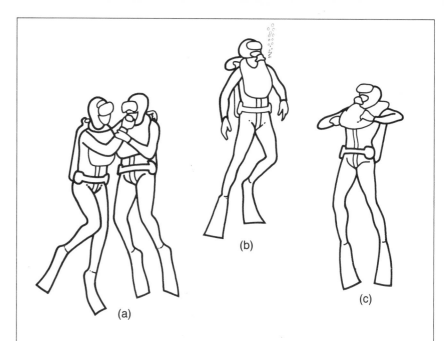

Emergency ascents. (a) An assisted ascent may be necessary if one diver runs out of air. He and his buddy surface while sharing air. (b) A free ascent involves finning to the surface while breathing out. Jettisoning the weightbelt may be necessary to begin the ascent. As the diver ascends the residual air in his lungs and in the cylinder should give him another mouthful of air. (c) A buoyant ascent uses the extra lift given by an inflated lifejacket. The diver inflates the jacket using a direct feed or compressed air from a separate cylinder. As he surfaces he should release air from the jacket by opening the dump valve to control his accelerating ascent rate.

give him four quick breaths of air, then inflate his lifejacket. You tow him to the shore (or a boat), continuing resuscitation. Finally, after landing him you carry out simulated cardiac massage.

### Emergency ascents

An *assisted ascent* is when a diver shares air with his buddy as they surface together (see p. 68). After the diver requiring help attracts his buddy's attention, he signals that he needs air. The 'donor' grabs his

harness strap and offers his regulator. A breathing pattern is established as the two divers ascend.

An assisted ascent is safer and more controlled than a free or buoyant ascent because the divers surface at a normal rate (15m per minute), and can even make decompression stops if necessary.

A *free ascent* is a dash to the surface, breathing out all the way. From depth, this can be dangerous because of the risk of the bends or

96

burst lung. It is only done by inexperienced or panicked divers, or when the correct buddy diving procedure has not been used.

A *buoyant ascent* in an emergency is like the free ascent, but faster because of the addition of an inflated lifejacket. This may cause the diver to surface at over 100m per minute. At such a speed, even if he breathes out hard all the way, there is a great risk of severely damaging his lungs *and* contracting the bends.

The air in the lifejacket will expand as the water pressure decreases. The diver's rate of ascent will therefore increase. If he is in a fit state to do so, he should vent the jacket during the ascent to slow him down.

If the dive should have included decompression stops, the diver should be watched carefully for symptoms of decompression sickness (see chapter 3), and taken to a recompression chamber if necessary.

A *controlled lift* is when an unconscious diver is brought to the surface, while buoyancy is controlled (see basic rescue procedure pp. 71-3).

## Diving from a boat

Launching an inflatable is a combined effort, requiring several willing hands. Once the inflatable is in the water, the bow is held pointing into the surf and the gear is loaded.

Inflatables can be very cramped when full of divers who are all trying to get kitted up. Except for your cylinder, you should keep your equipment in a bag. If it is only a short ride to the dive site, put on most of your gear before you get into the boat.

The skipper is in charge of the boat, and what he says must be respected. Inflatables are more efficient when loaded correctly, and it is up to the skipper to position you and your gear where he wants them. Sit down facing inwards on the inflated hull as soon as you get in.

Take a wind-proof jacket in cold conditions, as a wet suit will not give sufficient protection, particularly when the boat is skimming over the water and sending a spray of icy water onto your back.

At the dive site, the boatman monitors divers in and out of the water. But it is your job to keep a check on your own dive times, depths, etc.

On return to the beach, watch out for obstacles, such as swimmers or other boats. Again, on the skipper's command, some divers get out of the boat as it reaches the shore. They hold it steady while the others unload the equipment and stack it neatly, well clear of the waterline. Everyone then helps carry the boat up the beach.

## Underwater navigation

In the warm, crystal clear waters of the tropics it is possible to become disoriented and to lose your bearings. In cold, murky waters, losing your way is *probable* unless you plan your moves.

It is often important to be able to find your way back to a particular spot, such as the anchor line of your boat. The alternative is to surface, locate the boat, then waste energy swimming over to it, or else expect the crew to come and collect you. It is easier to start with a fixed point on the sea-bed, and to plan to return to it. This may be the anchor line or some distinctive feature, such as a wreck or unusual rock. When discussing the dive plan you will have established whether the skipper intends to remain anchored. If not, the anchor will not be there on your return.

As you fin away from the starting point, try to maintain a straight course, noting the formations you pass. Half way through the dive, turn through 180 degrees and pick out the same formations on your return journey to the anchor line.

Sometimes the sea floor is a continuous carpet of sand, rock or

An inflatable boat can be very cramped
when full of divers and their gear.

vegetation, and there are no
distinctive features by which to
navigate. This is when a magnetic
compass comes into its own. From
your starting point, face in the
direction you want to go and hold
the compass in front of you. The
needle will point to Magnetic North.
By setting the rotating bezel to
Magnetic North and keeping it
there as you swim along, you will
maintain the same course. Make

sure that a nearby steel cylinder or
ship wreck does not produce a
false reading from the compass.
For the return journey, turn around,
rotate the bezel through 180
degrees and repeat the exercise. In
calm water this will take you back
to your starting point. In a current
or tidal flow, you will be swept off
course, and must make
appropriate allowances.

Triangular or square courses can
be followed by taking a bearing

and finning in that direction for a
set time or number of fin strokes.
Keep checking that you are
following the correct bearing. Turn
through 120 degrees (in the case
of a triangle) or 90 degrees (for a
square), fin the same distance and
turn again. On a triangular course
this will then take you back to
where you started; on a square,
you need to repeat the process
once more to complete the fourth
side.

Beaching the boat.

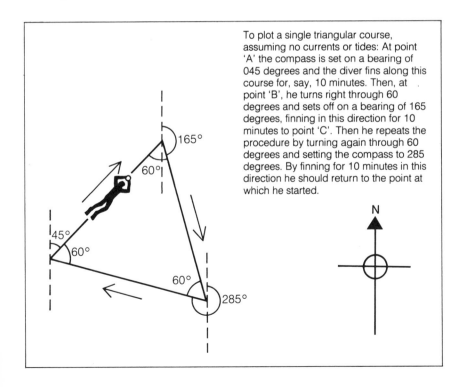

To plot a single triangular course, assuming no currents or tides: At point 'A' the compass is set on a bearing of 045 degrees and the diver fins along this course for, say, 10 minutes. Then, at point 'B', he turns right through 60 degrees and sets off on a bearing of 165 degrees, finning in this direction for 10 minutes to point 'C'. Then he repeats the procedure by turning again through 60 degrees and setting the compass to 285 degrees. By finning for 10 minutes in this direction he should return to the point at which he started.

# Surface marker buoy (SMB)

An SMB is usually a brightly-coloured, inflated float attached to a line which is held by one member of a buddy pair. The line is usually wound round a reel which the diver lets out as he descends and winds up as he ascends. It is a valuable aid, especially when you are diving in currents or poor visibility, as it tells those on the surface where you are. It will, for example, enable the dive boat to follow your movements and be waiting for you when you surface.

Some SMBs have a blue and white diving flag attached (see diagram), while a lamp is more suitable when on a night dive.

When you first take charge of the SMB, the line gets tangled in your fins on the way down, and you forget to wind it up when you ascend. The difficulties of controlling an SMB are discussed during the debriefing, and on the next dive you are careful to keep the line clear of your equipment, and wind it up as you ascend.

### Buddy line

In poor visibility divers risk becoming separated. This can be avoided by holding hands or by using a buddy line. It is thin but strong rope, maybe 2m long,

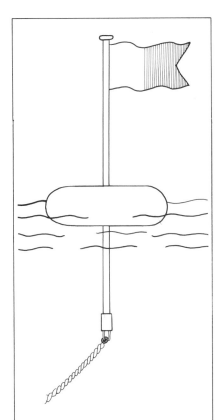

A surface marker buoy (SMB) is a float used to help people on the surface locate divers underwater. It is attached to the diver by a cord, which he unwinds from a reel as he descends and rewinds during ascent. Some buoys are fitted with the blue and white international code flag 'A' signifying 'Divers down. Keep clear'.

## Deep dives

Some divers think it is very clever to dive deep, and it is often these divers who find themselves in difficulties. Better wet suits, the popularity of dry suits and increased cylinder pressures have brought deep diving within the range of more sport divers. But still, the deeper you go, the colder and darker it becomes and the greater the risks of decompression sickness, nitrogen narcosis and other more insidious influences. A deep dive means a short dive and fewer dives in a day.

It is fine to view deep diving as a challenge, as long as you approach it in a level-headed manner, fully aware of the increased dangers. Many divers like to go below 30m once or twice simply to say they have done it. However, these dives must be carefully planned and even more meticulously monitored than usual, with constant checks on depth, time, air supply, your buddy and your own feelings (apprehension, light-headedness, etc). This is even more important when the water is cold and/or visibility is poor.

Do not expect to dive below 30m

looped around the wrist of both divers, or clipped to the lifejacket or harness to leave the hands free.

Inflating a surface marker buoy.

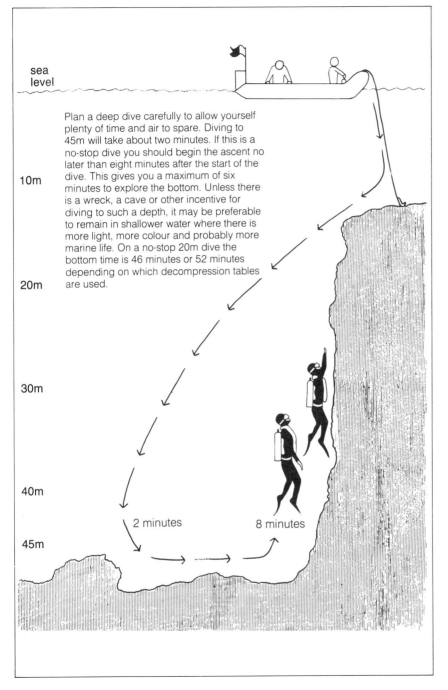

sea level

10m

20m

Plan a deep dive carefully to allow yourself plenty of time and air to spare. Diving to 45m will take about two minutes. If this is a no-stop dive you should begin the ascent no later than eight minutes after the start of the dive. This gives you a maximum of six minutes to explore the bottom. Unless there is a wreck, a cave or other incentive for diving to such a depth, it may be preferable to remain in shallower water where there is more light, more colour and probably more marine life. On a no-stop 20m dive the bottom time is 46 minutes or 52 minutes depending on which decompression tables are used.

30m

40m

45m

2 minutes

8 minutes

in the early stages of training. Build up to a deep dive so you become completely familiar with your equipment and your own reactions to depth. It is most important that you have a good, reliable regulator with a balanced valve which enables you to breathe easily even over 40m. An octopus rig is more likely to come into its own on a deep dive, where there is a higher risk of someone running out of air a long way from the surface.

Carry out a dummy run with stops at 10m and 5m to ensure that you can control buoyancy accurately enough. Then when you feel the time is right and you have found an experienced buddy you feel totally confident with, start making plans, taking into account the points made in this section.

To dive deep you should be fit, healthy and well-rested. Do not dive deep in rough conditions or where there is a tidal current which will drain your energy. Make sure you know where the nearest recompression chamber is, and how to get there. But plan the dive to avoid using it, as decompression sickness is painful and treatment is expensive. A fully kitted up support diver should be ready to enter the water at a moment's notice to assist a diver in distress or to take spare cylinders down to the level of the decompression stop.

Using the decompression tables

(explained later in this chapter) decide on the maximum depth and the time you are going to allow yourselves. No-stop dives — when you avoid having to decompress — are safer, more relaxed and there is no waiting around at 10m or 5m getting cold. If decompression stops are necessary, plan their depth and duration, and stick to your plan. If stops are not (or cannot be) made, through ignorance or shortage of air, the risk of decompression sickness is greatly increased. Calculate the amount of air you will need to complete the decompression stops, plus some extra in reserve. Synchronise watches and be accurate with the timings because every minute counts.

Different people react differently at depth, so, rather than diving to the limits recommended by the tables, build in a safety margin.

There is evidence to suggest that pregnant women should be able to continue diving, but should avoid decompression dives and not go deeper than 20m.

## Decreased buoyancy
On a deep dive, the gas bubbles in the neoprene of your diving suit are compressed more than on a shallow dive. Besides giving you less insulation against the cold, this decreases your buoyancy. If you are wearing too many weights, you

will have to put a lot of air into your ABLJ to compensate. Using the direct feed or ABLJ cylinder, inflate the jacket gradually as buoyancy decreases with depth. When you ascend, vent the jacket a little at a time, as you become more buoyant. If you are too buoyant, you will have difficulty staying at the level of decompression. Remember, you will be more buoyant at the end of the dive because the cylinder will be lighter.

## Contaminated air
The body can cope with small quantities of carbon dioxide or other contaminants breathed at the surface. But these toxic elements become more dangerous as pressure increases, and may lead to loss of consciousness. It is, therefore, most important that the compressor used to fill the air cylinders has effective filters and is properly managed to ensure a pure air supply.

## Rapid air consumption
As explained earlier, the air that you breathe from the cylinder when on a deep dive is much denser than on a shallow one. As a result the supply is depleted much faster; you consume approximately four times as much air at 30m as you do at the surface. It can be quite alarming to watch the needle on the contents gauge registering this

rapid depletion. Calculating the air requirement for a deep dive is therefore a critical element in the planning. Never plan to suck the air dry. Establish a regular, controlled breathing pattern to minimise the air consumption and make sure you have a good regulator. Allow a quarter of the cylinder's capacity as a reserve in case of emergency.

Air will also be used more quickly if you are cold, unfit, tense, apprehensive or particularly active. As these factors are hardly quantifiable, do not expect to put an exact figure on the amount of air you are going to use on a dive.

If you use 25 litres of air per minute at the surface, you will use 100 litres per minute at 30m. At this rate a 2,000 litre cylinder will be drained in 20 minutes. By leaving a quarter of the cylinder's capacity as a reserve, this is reduced to 15 minutes.

If you want to spend 30 minutes at 30m, you will obviously need more air than you would for 15 or 20 minutes. Breathing at a rate of 100 litres per minute, you will need 30 x 100 litres = 3,000 litres, plus 25% (reserve) = 750 litres. Therefore, the total capacity required = 3,750 litres. This means you will need two cylinders — perhaps a twin set (two cylinders mounted together) or access to a second cylinder during the dive.

In addition, a dive to such a

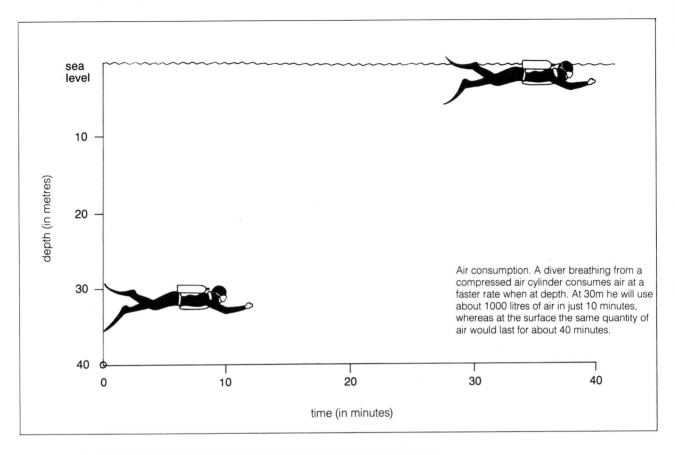

Air consumption. A diver breathing from a compressed air cylinder consumes air at a faster rate when at depth. At 30m he will use about 1000 litres of air in just 10 minutes, whereas at the surface the same quantity of air would last for about 40 minutes.

| Depth | Pressure | Rate of Air Consumption (based on 25 litres per minute at the surface) | Rate of Air Consumption (based on 35 litres per minute at the surface) |
|---|---|---|---|
| surface | 1 bar | 25 1/m | 35 1/m |
| 10m | 2 bar | 50 1/m | 70 1/m |
| 20m | 3 bar | 75 1/m | 105 1/m |
| 30m | 4 bar | 100 1/m | 140 1/m |
| 40m | 5 bar | 125 1/m | 175 1/m |
| 50m | 6 bar | 150 1/m | 210 1/m |

Air consumption varies from person to person. In addition, a diver needs more air if he is expending energy, or if he is cold or apprehensive. The average air consumption rate is 25 litres per minute at the surface.

depth for this length of time requires a decompression stop (see below). And because of the need for these stops, you cannot suddenly decide to return to the surface if you become apprehensive.

## Irrational behaviour
The psychological effects of depth should not be underestimated. Below 30m you are likely to become more anxious because you know you are a long way from the surface. If the visibility is poor, you may feel claustrophobic even if

you do not normally suffer. And maintaining buddy contact will be more difficult in poor visibility, giving rise to further cause for anxiety.

These symptoms are accentuated by nitrogen narcosis, outlined in chapter 3. The 'narcs' may induce slow reactions, irrational behaviour and unco-ordinated movements. If you are worried, tired, unfit or hung-over, you are more susceptible to the 'narcs'. And in this confused state you are more prone to making mistakes and causing accidents, and certainly incapable of helping your buddy if he gets into difficulty.

## Decompression tables

If you plan to dive deeper than 9m, it is essential that you understand how to use the decompression tables which indicate the limits of safe diving, beyond which the risk of suffering from decompression sickness — 'the bends' — is significantly increased.

Different diving organisations use different tables and different methods to calculate time allowed at depth. Some tables allow a smaller margin for error than others because they are based on different assumptions. Navy divers,

Timing a decompression stop.

for example, are better trained and fitter than the average sport diver, and have better back-up facilities. Their diving limits will therefore be extended, and sport divers should take this into account. You can easily put an end to your diving activities for ever for the sake of a few extra metres or minutes — always err on the side of safety.

On a decompression dive you will have to stop during the ascent to give the nitrogen time to come out of the tissues. While you are decompressing, it is much easier if you can hang onto a weighted shot-line or anchor line. If you are going to need more air because of the time spent decompressing, spare aqualungs can be tied to the line, a little deeper than the level at which you are going to stop. This should be viewed as an emergency air supply which will not be used if the dive goes according to plan. A fully-kitted support diver should be ready to enter the water at a moment's notice to assist a diver in distress. As he may be called on to go down to the deepest point of the dive he should have no time penalties against him.

For a single shallow dive of less than 9m (30ft), there is no danger of getting the bends and you do not need to refer to the table. If you are planning a deeper dive, where the ambient pressure is greater than 2 bar, you must be sure to remain within the limits of the table.

Special care must be taken if you dive more than once in one day because all the dives must be taken into account. Do the deep dive first and shallow one next. This is because a shallow first dive would penalise a deep second dive, giving you less bottom time. When the final dive is less than 9m (30ft) it carries no penalty. Note that the bottom time refers to the period from the beginning of the descent to the start of the ascent.

Printed here are examples drawn from the RNPL/BSAC (Royal Navy Physiological Laboratory/British Sub-Aqua Club) Decompression Table and the US Navy Decompression Table used by NAUI (The National Association of Underwater Instructors) and used by PADI (The Professional Association of Diving Instructors).

### RNPL/BSAC decompression table

The left-hand column refers to the maximum depth reached during the dive. The second column indicates the bottom time allowed at each depth without the need for a decompression stop. For example, you could dive to 18m for 57 minutes or to 40m for 11 minutes without stops.

If you include decompression stops you can stay at a given depth for longer. To calculate stop times find the depth of the dive in the left-hand column, say 18m, and move horizontally along that line until you reach the bottom time of the dive, say 66 minutes. Move down this column to the first white number on a black background. In this example the white number is 10. This means that a 18m dive with a bottom time of 66 minutes requires one 10 minute stop at 5m.

Dives deeper than 20m, which extend beyond the 'no-stop' limit, require two stops — one at 10m and the second at 5m. For example, take a 30m dive with a bottom time of 30 minutes. To calculate the decompression stops required find 30m in the left-hand column, follow the line along to 30 minutes, then down to the first white numbers on a black background. In this case the white numbers are 5 and 10, indicating the need for a 5-minute stop at 10m and a 10-minute stop at 5m. Note that the shallower stop is the longer one.

If the exact depth or time is not marked on the table, always over-estimate the depth or time spent underwater. For example, treat 29m as if it were 30m and 27 minutes as if it were 30 minutes.

After a dive deeper than 9m a certain amount of nitrogen will still be in the body even if the diver has remained within the limits of the tables. This is usually harmless and in time will dissipate. However, the

# RNPL/BSAC
# Decompression Table

1. Move down the **Maximum Depth** column to find the depth—or the next greater depth.
2. Move horizontally to find the **Bottom Time**—or the next greater time.
3. Move vertically down to read off any decompression **Stops** required.
4. Note that Maximum Depths greater than 20 m and requiring decompression involve a stop at 10 m and 5 m.
5. Dives to 9 m or less require no decompression.

| Maximum Depth metres | No Stop Time minutes | BOTTOM TIME IN MINUTES | | | | | |
|---|---|---|---|---|---|---|---|
| 10 | 232 | 431 | | | | | |
| 12 | 137 | 140 | 159 | 179 | 201 | 229 | 270 |
| 14 | 96 | 98 | 106 | 116 | 125 | 134 | 144 |
| 16 | 72 | 73 | 81 | 88 | 94 | 99 | 105 |
| 18 | 57 | 59 | 66 | 71 | 76 | 80 | 84 |
| 20 | 46 | 49 | 55 | 60 | 63 | 67 | 70 |
| Stops at 5 metres MINUTES | | 5 | 10 | 15 | 20 | 25 | 30 |

| Maximum Depth metres | No Stop Time minutes | | | | | |
|---|---|---|---|---|---|---|
| 22 | 38 | 42 | 47 | 51 | 55 | 58 |
| 24 | 32 | 37 | 41 | 45 | 48 | 51 |
| 26 | 27 | 32 | 37 | 40 | 43 | 45 |
| 28 | 23 | 29 | 33 | 36 | 39 | 41 |
| 30 | 20 | 25 | 30 | 33 | 35 | 37 |
| 32 | 18 | 23 | 27 | 30 | 32 | 34 |
| 34 | 16 | 21 | 25 | 28 | 30 | 31 |
| 36 | 14 | 20 | 23 | 26 | 27 | 29 |
| 38 | 12 | 18 | 21 | 24 | 26 | 27 |
| 40 | 11 | 17 | 20 | 22 | 24 | 25 |
| 42 | 10 | 16 | 19 | 21 | 22 | 24 |
| 44 | 9 | 15 | 18 | 20 | 21 | |
| 46 | 8 | 14 | 17 | 18 | 20 | |
| 48 | 8 | 13 | 16 | 17 | | |
| 50 | 7 | 12 | 15 | 17 | | |
| Stops at 10 metres MINUTES | | 5 | 5 | 5 | 5 | 5 |
| Stops at 5 metres | | 5 | 10 | 15 | 20 | 25 |

**Maximum Depth** is the greatest depth reached during dive.
**No Stop Time** is longest Bottom Time not requiring decompression stops.
**Bottom Time** is from start of descent to start of ascent.
**Descent Rate** is 30 metres/minute maximum.
**Ascent Rate** is 15 metres/minute.
**For More Than Two Dives** add bottom times together and decompress for greatest depth reached during dives.
**For Two Dives Only,** see opposite.
**No more than 8 hours in 24 spent under pressure (submerged).**

RNPL/BSAC air diving decompression table.

# Second Dives

When calculating decompression times for seond dives, **the greater depth of the two dives must be used.** The **Surface Interval** is the time from surfacing after the First Dive to descending for the Second Dive.
When **both** dives are shallower than 40 metres, the Time Penalty in Tabel A should be added to the Second Dive bottom time.

## TABLE A

| Surface Interval in hours | Time Penalty to be added to Second Dive bottom time |
|---|---|
| Less than 2 | All of First Dive bottom time |
| 2—4 | One half of First Dive bottom time |
| 4—6 | One Quarter of First Dive bottom time |
| More than 6 | No Time Penalty need be added |

When **either** dive is deeper than 40 metres, the Time Penalty in Table B should be added to the Second Dive bottom time.

## TABLE B

| Surface Interval in hours | Time Penalty to be added to Second Dive bottom time |
|---|---|
| Less than 2 | All of First Dive bottom time |
| 2— 4 | One half of First Dive bottom time |
| 4— 8 | One Quarter of First Dive bottom time |
| 8—16 | One eighth of First Dive bottom time |
| More than 16 | No Time Penalty need be added |

Second Dives to 9 metres or less carry no Time Penalty.

residual nitrogen still present in the body can have a cumulative effect if subsequent dives are made. Therefore a time penalty must be built in to the dive times.

If the last dive of the day is less than 9m it carries no penalty; you can go on a deep dive followed by as long as you like in water shallower than 9m.

For dives between 9m and 40m, refer to table A. For example, say the first dive has a maximum depth of 26m and bottom time of 20 minutes. To dive again within 2 hours of surfacing from the first dive you will have to add the entire 20 minutes of the first dive to the bottom time of the second dive. When calculating the timing for the second dive you must take the greater of the two depths — in this case 26m which allows a no-stop time of 27 minutes. If the second dive is to be a no-stop dive to 22m, you will have a bottom time of 27 minutes (total bottom time for both dives) minus 20 minutes (bottom time of the first dive), leaving 7 minutes.

No-stop time for max. depth of 26m = 27 minutes
Bottom time of first dive = 20 minutes
Bottom time allowed for second (no-stop) dive = 7 minutes

If you want (or need) to stay down for longer you will have to make decompression stops. For example, to stay down for 23 minutes on the second dive to 22m calculate the decompression times by adding the 20 minutes for the first dive to 23 minutes for the second dive, making a total of 43 minutes. Find 26m (max. depth) in the left-hand column of the table and look along the line until you reach 43 minutes. Next follow this column down to the white numbers on a black background which tell you to decompress for 5 minutes at 10m and 20 minutes at 5m.

Leaving a longer interval between dives means you have to add only a proportion of the bottom time of the first dive. For an interval of 2 - 4 hours add a half of the first bottom time. For an interval of 4 - 6

hours add a quarter of the first bottom time. Beyond 6 hours no penalty need be added to the bottom time of the second dive.

When either dive is deeper than 40m time penalties must be added even when the interval between dives is greater than 6 hours. See table B. For example, a first dive to 42m has a bottom time of 16 minutes, involving stops of 5 minutes at 10m and 5m. If the second dive takes place after, say, 3 hours, 8 minutes (half of 16 minutes) must be added to the bottom time of the second dive. If the second dive takes place after an interval of 15 hours (which could be the following day), 2 minutes (one eighth of 16 minutes) must be added.

For three or more dives add the bottom times together and decompress for the greatest depth reached.

Make sure you understand the table by working out the following examples:
1. You want to dive for an hour at 20m. Will you have to decompress and, if so, for how long and at what depth?
2. What is the greatest bottom time you can allow yourself on a 30m dive without needing to stop during the ascent?
3. On a 45m dive your bottom time is 18 minutes. What are your decompression stops?

4. Your first dive to 28m has a bottom time of 10 minutes. What interval should you leave before making a 'no-stop' dive of 18 minutes to 22m?
5. You have made a 48m decompression dive with a bottom time of 16 minutes. After 7 hours you want to dive to 26m and are only prepared to decompress for a total of 10 minutes. What is the maximum bottom time you can allow yourself on the second dive?
Answers on page 110.

## US Navy decompression table
The left-hand column of table 1 refers to the maximum depth of the dive. To find the 'no-stop' time of a dive to 80ft, locate 80 in the left-hand column and follow the line horizontally until you reach a circle. The number in the circle is the 'no-stop' time in minutes — in this case 40 minutes.

If you increase your bottom time to 50 minutes, the figures printed under '50' indicate that you have to decompress for 10 minutes at 10ft. And for a bottom time of 60 minutes you would decompress for 17 minutes at 10ft.

The maximum 'no-stop' time for a 100ft dive is 25 minutes. A 100ft dive with a bottom time of 30 minutes requires a stop of 3 minutes at 10ft. And a bottom time of 40 minutes requires a 15-minute stop at 10ft.

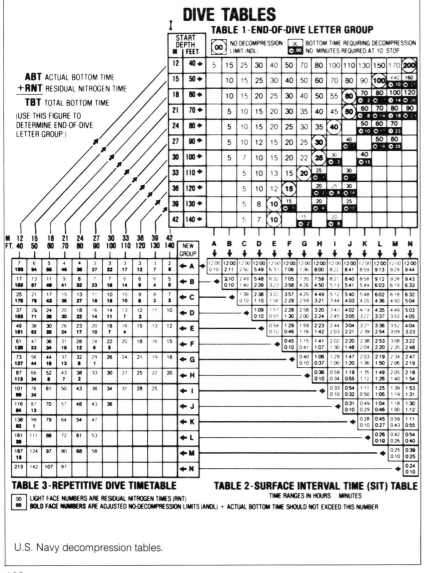

**DIVE TABLES**

**TABLE 1 - END-OF-DIVE LETTER GROUP**

ABT ACTUAL BOTTOM TIME
+RNT RESIDUAL NITROGEN TIME
TBT TOTAL BOTTOM TIME
(USE THIS FIGURE TO DETERMINE END-OF-DIVE LETTER GROUP)

**TABLE 3 - REPETITIVE DIVE TIMETABLE**

LIGHT FACE NUMBERS ARE RESIDUAL NITROGEN TIMES (RNT)
BOLD FACE NUMBERS ARE ADJUSTED NO-DECOMPRESSION LIMITS (ANDL) · ACTUAL BOTTOM TIME SHOULD NOT EXCEED THIS NUMBER

**TABLE 2 - SURFACE INTERVAL TIME (SIT) TABLE**

TIME RANGES IN HOURS     MINUTES

U.S. Navy decompression tables.

After one dive, a diver using this system allocates himself a letter which relates to the amount of residual nitrogen in his body. The higher the residual nitrogen, the later in the alphabet the letter is. For example, to find out what letter to give himself after an 80ft dive with a bottom time of 30 minutes he looks along the line in table 1 from 80ft until he reaches 30, then down that column to the letter 'G'. Therefore after this dive he is a 'G' diver.

This letter grade comes into its own for subsequent dives. After surfacing, the nitrogen slowly dissipates and the diver's letter grading changes. Table 2 is the surface interval time table. From the letter 'G' at the top of table 2 look down to the bottom of the column. Two figures, 0.10 and 0.40 are written one above the other. These indicate an interval between dives of between 10 and 40 minutes. Now follow the arrow to the left until you reach 'G' in table 3. This means that between 10 and 40 minutes after surfacing from the first dive, the diver is still a 'G' diver.

Go back to the 'G' column on table 2 and find 0.41 and 1.15, which refers to a surface interval of between 41 minutes and 1 hour 15 minutes. Now follow the line to the left to table 3 which shows that after such an interval a diver becomes

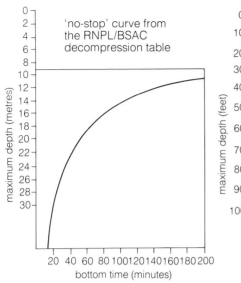

'no-stop' curve from the RNPL/BSAC decompression table

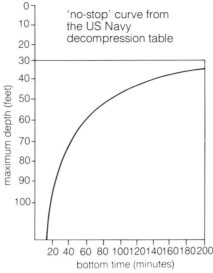

'no-stop' curve from the US Navy decompression table

The curve shows the length of time you can dive without needing to stop during the ascent and decompress. If you dive beyond the limits of the 'no-stop' curve you must follow the decompression table and stop to allow time for the nitrogen to be dispelled. If in any doubt whether or not you have exceeded the 'no-stop' limit, then stop for at least 5 minutes at a depth of 5m.

Aqualung divers do not need to stop and decompress on ascent as long as the bottom time does not exceed the time shown in this table.

| RNPL/BSAC | | US Navy | |
|---|---|---|---|
| max. depth (m) | bottom time (mins) | max. depth (ft) | bottom time (mins) |
| 9 | no limit | 30 | no limit |
| 10 | 232 | 40 | 200 |
| 12 | 137 | 50 | 100 |
| 14 | 96 | 60 | 60 |
| 16 | 72 | 70 | 50 |
| 18 | 57 | 80 | 40 |
| 20 | 46 | 90 | 30 |
| 22 | 38 | 100 | 25 |
| 24 | 32 | | |
| 26 | 27 | | |
| 28 | 23 | | |
| 30 | 20 | | |

an 'F' diver. With an interval of between 1 hour 16 minutes and 1 hour 59 minutes he becomes an 'E' diver. With an interval of between 2 hours and 2 hours 58 minutes he becomes a 'D' diver, and so on.

The bold figures in table 3 show

that if he is still a 'G' diver, his second 'no-stop' dive to 80ft can have a maximum bottom time of only 8 minutes. As an 'F' diver a second 'no-stop' dive to 80ft has a bottom time of 12 minutes. A 'B' diver has 32 minutes, and so on.

To become a 'B' diver after a first dive which made you a 'G' diver, you must leave an interval of between 4 hours 26 minutes and 7 hours 35 minutes.

Above the bold figures on table 3 (the no-stop dive times) are numbers which refer to the residual nitrogen times (RNT). The RNT is the time the diver should consider he has *already* spent on the bottom when he *starts* a repeat dive to a specific depth. Adding the two figures together gives the total no-stop time for a particular depth. Confirm this by returning to table 1 and finding the no-stop time for that depth (the number in a circle).

For example, if an 'E' diver on his second dive goes to 80ft (see table 2) he should consider he has already spent 23 minutes on the bottom. At 80ft he now has a no-stop bottom time of 17 minutes. Add the two figures: 23 + 17 = 40. Return to table 1 and find the circled number which is the no-stop time for a dive to 80ft, i.e. 40 minutes.

If this 'E' diver wants to dive to 80ft for longer than 17 minutes he will have to make a decompression stop. To find out the stop time on, say, a 37-minute second dive, add the residual nitrogen time, 23 minutes, to the length of the second dive, 37 minutes, making 60 minutes. Then on table 1 look along the line from 80ft to 60 minutes. This indicates a decompression stop of 17 minutes at 10ft.

Try the following examples:

6. Does a 60ft dive with a bottom time of 60 minutes require a decompression stop?

7. What is the stop time for a 70ft dive with a bottom time of 60 minutes?

8. After a 90ft dive with a bottom time of 25 minutes what grade of diver are you?

9. If the 25-minute 90ft dive is your first dive, what interval must you leave before you become a 'C' diver?

10. As a 'C' diver, what is the maximum bottom time you can allow yourself on a 70ft no-stop dive?

Answers opposite.

## Diving at altitude

As you climb a mountain ambient pressure decreases below 1 bar. You must compensate for this when calculating the depth of a dive in a mountain lake or quarry. Add the following penalty to the depth:

| Altitude | To depth gauge reading |
|---|---|
| 100-300m | add a quarter of depth indicated |
| 300-2000m | add a third of depth indicated |
| 2000-3000m | add a half of depth indicated |

## Flying after a dive

If you go up a mountain or fly in an aircraft straight after a deep dive, you are subjecting your body to decreased pressure, which may bring on decompression sickness. If the dive involved any decompression stops, you should allow 24 hours before flying. If there were no stops, allow at least two hours.

Answers to decompression questions on pages 107 and 110.

1. Yes, for 15 minutes at 5m.
2. 20 minutes.
3. 5 minutes at 10m and 15 minutes at 5m.
4. 2 - 4 hours.
5. 13 - 4 = 9 minutes.
6. No.
7. 8 minutes at 10ft.
8. A 'G' diver.
9. 2 hours 59 minutes - 4 hours 25 minutes.
10. 35 minutes.

*Note:*
The British Sub-Aqua Club has commissioned a new set of dive tables, but these were not available at the time of going to press.

# 7. Types of dive

Part of the attraction of diving is the tremendous variety you can experience below the surface of the ocean. This variety is multiplied when you start going on different types of dive. Those who restrict themselves to one or two types of diving are not getting the most out of their sport.

Sometimes the type of dive will be governed largely by the conditions at the dive site. For example, it would be dangerous to dive at night in a five-knot current. The aim of the dive in this case should be clear — dive during the day and enjoy the sensation of a drift dive!

Accept, too, that conditions can change, and adapt accordingly. What looked like being a calm sea with clear visibility, ideal for photography, may turn murky. In which case it may be better to leave your camera packed away.

Even if the aim of the dive is a fairly vague one, such as 'to have a general look around', the buddy pair should still agree on a dive plan: who will lead? which way first? what maximum depth? when to begin the ascent? And once the dive has started, stick to the plan. If you are at 35m and suddenly decide that it would be fun to go down a further 10m, remember, you may be acting under the influence of nitrogen narcosis!

Dives in deep, cold water, where the surface is choppy and a current is trying to sweep you away, are physically demanding and should be attempted only by those in peak condition. Always remain within your capabilities, and if necessary keep to shallower, more sheltered waters.

## River diving

Diving in rivers can be rewarding, because of what you see *and* what you retrieve, but you should be aware of certain hazards. Generally, the current is slower at the edges of a river due to friction with the bed and banks. Do not be deceived by the calm water near the sides; the flow in the middle might be faster than you can cope with. Consider, too, your point of exit. Where will you get out if you are swept downstream?

The flow of the water churns up sediment on the river bed, especially after heavy rains. Add to this the disruptive action of a pair of energetic fins, and visibility may be reduced to a few centimetres. Near centres of population you must be particularly wary of old bikes and bedsteads, twisted metal and even cars. Murky urban rivers are also more likely to be polluted and carry bacteria which can give you an infection. Avoid locks and sluice gates which can drag you down or trap you.

Despite the obstacles, some divers relish the opportunity to dive for old bottles, coins, knives or whatever. It is also a chance to help out boatmen by retrieving lost anchors, ropes, and so on.

As long as you have not chosen to dive in polluted waters, you will see a surprising amount of aquatic life, such as pike, perch and eels.

Do not overweight yourself. Remember, you are less buoyant in fresh water, and therefore need fewer weights.

## Beach diving

Walking into the water from a beach can be the easiest way to dive: no need to organise a boat and no bumpy ride out to the dive site. Yet there is a technique to enjoying a beach dive.

Choose a beach where the entry to the water is sheltered and free from obstacles. The ideal is a gently shelving beach, clear of harbour walls and other potential hazards.

In a moderate surf, you will have a tiring time battling through with all your gear. And when you finally start the dive, visibility is likely to be poor because of the turbulence. Inflate your lifejacket enough to give you some buoyancy. Then walk backwards into the shallow water; it is much easier than trying to walk forwards with fins on. When

Walk backwards when entering the water from the beach.

the water is about a metre deep, turn around and let yourself go out with the backwash, then stand your ground when a breaker tries to take you up the beach again. But take care, you can damage yourself or your equipment by being knocked

over by a wave, and it is difficult to get up again while carrying a heavy cylinder. It is often better to lie face down as early as you can, and breathe through your regulator while crawling or finning out along the surface. That way the water

takes the weight of your gear, you don't. Once beyond the breakers, replace your regulator with a snorkel to conserve air, or begin the dive.

Coming in at the end of the dive is easier as you can ride the waves

Everyone lends a hand loading dive gear onto the boat.

## Boat diving

Entering the water from a boat avoids some of the hazards associated with a beach dive. A boat enables you to dive further from the shore, perhaps exploring deeper waters or ship wrecks beyond the normal range of a shore dive. Small inflatable boats can be fast and manoeuvrable, and they are sufficiently inexpensive to be within the budget of many dive clubs.

until it is shallow enough to stand and walk in backwards.

If the surf is strong, with waves over a metre high, you would be wise to cancel the dive or look elsewhere.

The blue and white 'A' flag indicates that divers are down.

While divers are in the water the blue and white International Code Flag 'A' should be displayed to warn other vessels to keep their distance. This 'Diver Down' flag is also used on surface marker buoys. While divers are down, the boat's motor should be in neutral, except when on the way to pick up divers.

Orange and red parachute flares should be carried in the boat to attract attention when in difficulty, and should be used only in an emergency.

For a more comfortable ride out to a dive site, a larger boat has many advantages over a small inflatable one. A dive club may hire a boat and skipper, or you might join a dive operation which has its own hardboat. Many diving holidays are based on specially equipped dive boats (see chapter 9).

Besides stability, a large boat gives you more space in which to store your gear and to move around. You do not need to get fully kitted up before you board as this can be done when you arrive at the site. Specially equipped boats have racks where you can store your cylinders safely and out of the way.

A ladder over the side of the boat makes boarding easy. Take your fins off before climbing the ladder.

Plan your dive to return to the boat, rather than expecting the boat to come and pick you up, unless there is a good reason to arrange otherwise.

Most boats used for diving have a sturdy ladder or even a platform at water level, which makes getting in and out relatively easy. Although it is fun jumping off the boat from a great height, you risk hurting yourself or losing items of equipment. By descending down the anchor line, you can assess the strength and direction of the current, and you have a fixed point to return to at the end of the dive. A weighted stern line or shot-line with 5m and 10m markers is useful if divers are planning decompression stops. The more luxurious boats have carpeted areas which wet divers should avoid.

Remember, the skipper's word is law and should be respected. Other members of the party, besides the skipper, should know how to operate the radio, start the engine and perform basic manoeuvres with the boat.

## Wreck diving

Wrecks in calmer or deeper waters remain intact much longer than exposed, shallow water wrecks, which are more vulnerable to storm damage and therefore more prone to breaking up and being strewn

A platform at the back of the boat takes much of the effort out of entering and leaving the water.

A knife and torch are essential aids to exploring a wreck. Use your knife to cut yourself free from snagged fishing lines and nets. Wear a wet suit and gloves for protection against jagged metal, wires and ropes. Take extra care when investigating a frail, crumbling wreck. Avoid kicking up sediment, as this will reduce visibility. Treat the inside of a wreck as a cave, and use a line attached across the sea-bed. What was once a maritime disaster becomes a marine playground — open only to divers. An amazing collection of marine life is attracted to a wreck within days of its appearance on the sea-bed. While these flourishing colonies fascinate some divers, trophy-hunters, being more acquisitive than inquisitive, set about stripping bits of brass or searching out other treasures to adorn their homes. Remember though, that all wrecks belong to *someone*. In theory you should obtain permission before salvaging anything.

A disaster at sea becomes a playground for wreck divers.

On a large purpose-built dive boat there is usually plenty of room to stow gear and get kitted up without kicking someone in the face!

to your buddy outside to prevent getting lost. It is easy to become engrossed in what you are doing. Keep looking at your watch and give yourself plenty of time to leave the wreck and surface at the end of the dive.

## Drift diving

In certain places around the world, the current is too rapid for you to be able to stay in one place without a great deal of effort. Sometimes the speed of the current is increased by an ebbing or flooding tide being forced between two land masses. Rapid currents (over 10 knots) are too dangerous for the sport diver, but a moderate current (4 - 6 knots) can provide an

exhilarating dive, as long as it is carefully thought out and has good surface cover.

Drift dives are always conducted from a boat. You are dropped at one point, with a group of divers, one of whom has a surface marker buoy (SMB). You descend to the agreed depth, perhaps down a reef wall or cliff face, while also being swept along by the current. Using your fins as rudders to steer,

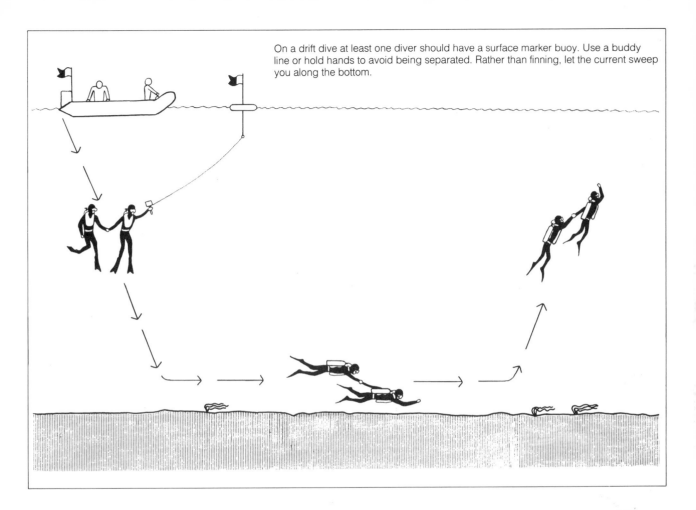

On a drift dive at least one diver should have a surface marker buoy. Use a buddy line or hold hands to avoid being separated. Rather than finning, let the current sweep you along the bottom.

you fly past the submarine scenery with the minimum of effort, and only have time for a fleeting glimpse. Eddies and mini-whirlpools massage your body in a three-dimensional waterslide/Jacuzzi.

As the average diver can fin along at a maximum of about three knots for short bursts, it is almost impossible to retrieve a dropped knife or snorkel. However, friction with the sea-bed slows the current,

and it is often possible to find nooks and crannies where the water is calm. Remaining in a group can be difficult as everything happens so quickly and you have little control over where you go. Holding hands with your buddy or using a buddy line are the best ways to avoid being separated.

Meanwhile, the dive boat follows the SMB, and should be close at hand when you all surface.

## Diving in the tropics

For some, diving in clear, warm waters, surrounded by multicoloured fish and strange-shaped corals is the only way to dive. It is here you see turtles, manta rays and giant grouper. And it is here that you can dive safely with white tipped reef sharks and moray eels. The attractions are certainly tempting.

117

Hitching a ride on a passing turtle.

A moray eel can inflict a nasty bite on an unwary diver.

Because it is warmer and clearer in tropical waters, you are likely to be more relaxed, physically and mentally. Your body does not have to work so hard coping with the cold, and you are less anxious about possible hidden dangers. But do not let the clarity of the water lure you deeper than the dive tables allow. When the water is clear, there is a tendency to dive deep without realising it, yet the risks of decompression sickness, nitrogen narcosis and rapid air consumption are ever-present. Just because your body is relaxed, do not relax your vigilance — continue checking your depth and contents gauges, keep an eye on the time and maintain good buddy diving procedure. You may be able to *see* your buddy 15m away, but how long would it take you to reach him in the event of an emergency?

When the water temperature is over 20°C, you can dive quite happily for a short while without a wet suit, especially if you are warm to start with and can return to brilliant sunshine after the dive. In the tropics water temperatures can reach 30°C, yet it is often a good idea to wear a thin (4mm) or shortie wet suit to protect your body from a variety of aquatic nasties. Fire coral

Maintain good buddy diving procedure even in clear tropical waters.

Stone fish are very difficult to see, yet they have stingers on their upper dorsal fins which contain strong poison.

Stings and burns should be treated with alcohol, antihistamine, lemon juice or vinegar.

The smaller creatures are generally more irksome than sharks, which are sometimes curious, but generally keep their distance. Sharks are more interested in a person or sea creature thrashing about in the water. For this reason, swimmers and snorkellers are more at risk than divers. Sharks are also attracted to blood, so if you have cut yourself or have caught a fish, leave the water promptly.

Dangers out of the water should also be considered. By not protecting yourself from sunburn, you may find it too painful to put on

can give you a burning rash, which may irritate for days. Some sponges and plant-like hydroids can give a painful sting. The stone fish, scorpion fish, lion fish and certain jellyfish can inflict an excruciating, sometimes fatal, wound. If you enter the water from the beach and have nothing on your feet, be on the look out for sea urchins. Their spines are barbed and very difficult to remove if they break off in your foot. If you do not get them out, they can soon become infected.

Fire lion fish or butterfly cod have large fan-like pectoral fins and poisonous spines on their dorsal fins.

Night dive from the beach.

diving procedure. Make sure that the surface cover knows when you are expected to return so they are ready to act if you are overdue. Choose an entry and exit point without obstacles. Mark your exit point with a light, whether it is on the beach or a boat. Do not dive deeper than about 15m.

Everyone on a night dive should have a good source of light, not only to illuminate the flowering corals and nocturnal predators, but also to avoid bumping into things.

Before the dive, do not wave torches around, as this does nothing to improve your ability to see in the dark, and it may be interpreted by the coastguard as a distress signal.

Once safely on the bottom, it is an enchanting experience to turn off all your lights and 'feel' the atmosphere. It is surprising how much can be seen underwater at night when your eyes have adapted to the dark. Then, rather than trying to cover a lot of distance, with the risk of getting lost, stay in one area and watch the details of the marine life around you.

Torches should be kept on at all times during the dive, other than for the planned 'black-out'. Besides bringing out the true colours of the undersea world, a light enables you to keep in touch with your buddy and to find the torch if it is

diving equipment. When snorkelling in the middle of the day wear a T-shirt. Insect bites can also be annoying. Use antihistamine cream to soothe irritation.

# Night dives

At night the underwater world changes dramatically. It is feeding time and the hunters emerge to stalk their prey. Spiders and shrimps leave their tubular sponges in search of food, coral polyps extend beyond their cretaceous shelters to catch micro-organisms in the water and the moray eel

leaves its shelter to look for its midnight feast.

Your first night dive can be a nerve-tingling experience. Visibility, which may have been excellent by day, is reduced to a narrow tunnel of light provided by your torch. Your senses are sharpened; your breathing seems louder; swaying kelp looks ominous; and an innocent brush against a rock seems threatening.

Unless you feel confident and secure, night diving can be unsettling, instead of fascinating. You should therefore plan the dive very carefully and stick to buddy dropped. You can attract attention by waving the light around, but do not shine it into your buddy's eyes, as he will not thank you for destroying his night vision! Give signals by shining the torch at your hand. If one light fails, a buddy pair should surface holding hands to avoid separation.

On surfacing, a single stationary beam directed towards the boat or surface cover means 'OK'. Rapid waving of the torch beam means 'Something is wrong, come and collect us'. Warm clothing and a hot drink are especially welcome after a night dive.

## Blue hole diving

Blue holes are deep hollows, sometimes found in the sea, sometimes inland. Some of the best examples of blue holes are found in the Bahamas. Unfortunately, there is usually a strong current associated with the ebb of the tide, when water is sucked down into the hole. This can prove an insurmountable hazard for the diver, and blue holes should be approached with caution.

## Diving under ice

Diving under ice can be very exciting but also very hazardous, and special precautions must be taken.

Again, advanced planning is the hallmark of success. The cold is the first consideration. In temperatures of less than 10°C, make sure you start off warm and, for preference, wear a dry suit to minimise the risk of hypothermia.

On some regulators you can clip a flexible rubber winterising cap, containing an antifreeze mixture. This helps stop the first stage of the regulator from freezing.

Only dive under stationary ice, as moving ice can quickly block your line of retreat. Surface cover should include at least one experienced, fully kitted-up diver and two experienced divers, each in charge of one member of the buddy pair. A life-line should be attached to one of the divers, under his equipment, linking him with his surface cover. And a buddy line should also join the two buddies. More than two divers down at any one site is likely to create an unhelpful tangle of lines. Communication between diver and the surface can be done by tugging on the line. Line signals are explained in chapter 8. Always return to the surface with plenty of air.

## Cave diving

Cave diving is a potentially dangerous pastime requiring steely nerves, good back-up and

specialised training, which can be gained by joining a cave diving organisation. Most cave divers are cavers who want to extend the range of their caving activities. They have therefore borrowed diving techniques and adapted these to their needs.

A cave diver usually wears one cylinder on each side, mounted on the hips. A cylinder on the back is vulnerable to damage and makes it hard to squeeze through narrow passages. A helmet has two or three lights attached. A lifeline on a reel links the cave diver with his point of entry, and if he loses this, finding the way out of a labyrinth of tunnels can soon develop into a nightmare. If equipment fails or the air runs out, there is no chance of a quick escape to the surface. Cave divers therefore take with them spares of everything. They begin their return journey when they have used just a third of their air supply. That way, they should emerge with an additional third still in the cylinder, essential in case of emergency.

# 8. Associated skills

By the time you have completed your basic training and have been on a variety of open-water dives, it is easy to become over-confident and begin to relax the rules. But it is now more important than ever that you understand the rules of the game ... and keep to them.

You may want to show off by going deeper than everyone else, or by staying down on your own at the end of a dive. But the measure of a good diver is *not* assessed by how far he tries to push the limits of the sport. A good diver is someone who sticks to the correct code of practice, does not take unnecessary risks, and considers diving as much a discipline as a skill.

### The experienced diver
As you become more experienced, the mechanics of diving will become second nature to you and you will not have to devote your full attention to yourself and your equipment. You may then be placed in charge of one or more less experienced divers. If so, you must not only set a good example, but also be sensitive to their needs, ensuring that they have an enjoyable, trouble-free dive.

The more experienced you are, the more observant you should be, and the more able to assess the significance of what you see. Formulate a plan based on the

value you place on what is happening. For example, if you notice that your buddy seems unusually concerned about his mask or is having difficulty clearing his ears, react accordingly. Give him plenty of time to sort himself

out, keep checking that he is all right, and, if necessary, return with him to the surface.

Once you have mastered the basics of diving, you will want to find ways of broadening your diving activities. You can begin to develop new interests and skills, some of which will be discussed in this chapter.

Keep your own skills polished. It is good practice to perform various exercises underwater with your buddy, to keep you up to scratch at all times. For example, when did you last take off your mask underwater to make sure you can breathe easily without water going up your nose? Try buddy breathing from time to time, and, in controlled conditions, a simulated rescue.

Without constant practice, skills soon become rusty.

## Planning a dive

Every dive, however modest, should be carefully planned and prepared. To avoid confusion arising from conflicting instructions, there should be one person in charge, whether the dive involves two people or 20. It is his job to co-ordinate the dive and take responsibility for any incidents.

### Planning procedure
○ Select the location of the dive. It may be a known site, one recommended by other divers, one described in a book or magazine, or a virgin site about which you know very little.
○ Decide on the main purpose of the dive. This may be to train novice divers, explore a wreck, take photographs, discover new territory, etc.
○ Decide when the dive should take place. Obviously it should be at a time which is convenient for those who want to dive, but consider, too, such factors as the time of day, tides, weather conditions, etc.
○ Arrange for boat hire and, where necessary, obtain permission to dive at a particular site well in advance.
○ Check all equipment is in test and ready for the dive, including the boat.
○ Keep a record of who is involved with the dive, their telephone number, diving experience, etc.
○ Check that all divers are suitably qualified.
○ Consider weather forecasts on the radio, TV or in the paper. If necessary, phone the Meteorological Office. This may save you the expense of travelling to the site, and then finding the conditions are too bad for diving.
○ Examine maps and charts for suitable access points, depths, wrecks, rocks, etc.
○ Ensure adequate transportation.
○ Assess the state of the tide by studying tide tables, and, where possible, draw on local knowledge of conditions, especially if the dive is one which should be carried out in slack water.
○ Have a note of the telephone number of emergency services, including the coastguard, doctor and nearest recompression chamber. Know where the nearest telephone is.
○ Make sure you know how to reach the nearest recompression chamber.
○ Ensure that an adequate first aid kit is brought.
○ Alert the local coastguard of your dive plan.
○ Contact everyone concerned if arrangements are changed.
○ Inform everyone of dive times and encourage people to keep to them.

### On the day
○ Observe the divers' code of conduct (see below).
○ Give a pre-dive briefing, outlining the aim of the dive and any special conditions.
○ Make a note of the time each diver enters the water.
○ When the divers surface, note the maximum depth and bottom time of each diver.
○ Make provision for the divers' comfort after the dive. This may involve finding somewhere warm and dry, with warm or energy-giving food.

## Divers' code of conduct

○ Make sure the impression you leave with other beach users is a good one. Remember, divers are conspicuous.
○ Locate the compressor away from people who may be disturbed by its noise.
○ Keep gear contained, not spread over the beach, and do not leave litter.
○ Be polite and obey local rules and regulations.
○ Do not obstuct or interfere with other people's use of the beach or sea.
○ Dive away from fishermen's nets, buoys or pots, unless you have an opportunity to help by retrieving their gear.

### Conservation

○ Especially in well-used sites, marine life is in danger of being severely depleted by non-thinking divers.
○ Do not collect young crabs, lobsters, etc., and take only what you intend to eat.
○ Do not use a speargun with scuba gear.
○ Discourage marine pollution or damage to the undersea environment.
○ Take only photos and notes, leave only bubbles.

## Tide tables

Tides ebb and flow in response to the forces of the moon and sun. The amount of change varies around the world. The greatest tidal range occurs a day or two after new and full moon (every 15 days), when the gravitational pull is strongest. This is called the *Spring tide* and it produces the highest and lowest water levels. In some locations the difference between high and low tide can be as much as 17m, while in others it is less than 1m.

The smallest tidal range occurs between two Spring tides, and is called the *Neap tide*.

Unless you are planning a drift dive, using tidal currents, aim for the period of slack water — usually either side of high or low tide, although local variations do occur.

In many countries tide tables are available in nautical books or as a separate booklet. They are produced for selected ports and times given may be a few minutes different from the times at your dive site.

## Maritime charts

A chart is a map of an area of the sea. It can be small scale, showing, say, a detailed plan of a harbour, or large scale, covering an entire ocean. Charts are intended primarily to assist mariners with navigation, but there is much information of use to divers. Water depth, condition of the sea-bed, wreck location and tidal streams are all shown. One of the most popular series of charts is that produced by the UK Government as Admiralty Charts. These are metric charts, with depths marked in metres rather than the traditional fathoms.

Consider the following points when reading a chart:
○ *Directions* Charts are drawn to align with the lines of latitude and longitude, such that the sides of the chart point to the North Pole. But a compass points to Magnetic North, somewhere in northern Canada. Magnetic North moves around and the *variation* from True North changes from year to year, but the change is only minor, and seldom affects divers.
○ *Depths* The depth shown on a chart is relative to *Chart Datum*, which is the lowest water level ever recorded, and is marked on many harbour walls. At high water there may be a much greater depth at the dive site than the number printed on the chart. It is possible to recalculate the depth at the site by checking the tide tables and assessing the state of the tide at

| Place | Lat N | Long W | Heights in metres above datum | | | |
|---|---|---|---|---|---|---|
| | | | MHWS | MHWN | MLWN | MLWS |
| Coverack | 50 01 | 5 05 | 5.3 | 4.2 | 1.9 | 0.6 |

The tidal range at Springs is greater than that at Neaps. The Mean High Water Springs (MHWS) at Coverack is 5.3m above the datum line. Springs low tide (MLWS) is 0.6m. Neaps tides range from 1.9m to 4.2m above datum.

| | | ◇ E | 50°02'.4N 5 02.3W | | ◇ F | 50°02'.5N 4 58.7W | |
|---|---|---|---|---|---|---|---|
| Hours | | Dir | Rate (kn) Sp Np | | Dir | Rate (kn) Sp Np | |
| Before HW | 6 | 201 | 1.0 | 0.5 | 215 | 1.0 | 0.5 |
| | 5 | 309 | 0.1 | 0.0 | 220 | 0.5 | 0.2 |
| | 4 | 006 | 1.0 | 0.5 | 293 | 0.1 | 0.1 |
| | 3 | 011 | 1.4 | 0.7 | 017 | 0.5 | 0.2 |
| | 2 | 015 | 1.5 | 0.8 | 029 | 0.9 | 0.5 |
| | 1 | 022 | 1.5 | 0.7 | 043 | 1.2 | 0.6 |
| HW | | 028 | 1.2 | 0.6 | 043 | 1.2 | 0.6 |
| After HW | 1 | 030 | 0.5 | 0.2 | 040 | 0.7 | 0.4 |
| | 2 | 202 | 0.4 | 0.2 | Slack | | |
| | 3 | 196 | 1.2 | 0.6 | 214 | 0.5 | 0.3 |
| | 4 | 195 | 1.7 | 0.9 | 210 | 0.9 | 0.5 |
| | 5 | 197 | 1.6 | 0.8 | 213 | 1.3 | 0.6 |
| | 6 | 202 | 1.2 | 0.6 | 216 | 1.2 | 0.6 |

Each diamond containing a capital letter provides the key to the speed and direction of the current at a specific location. For example, find the diamond with the letter F. Direction (Dir) is given as a bearing from Magnetic North. The table above shows that at high water (HW) the tidal stream is flowing towards 043 magnetic (approximately north-east). Speed is given in knots (Rate kn). At Springs (Sp) its speed is 1.2 knots; at Neaps (Np) its speed is 0.6 knots. The main slack period occurs 2 hours after HW.

◀ A section of an Admiralty Chart showing depths marked in metres, referring to the depth at the lowest water level. The segment of the compass rose shows Magnetic North as 7° 35'W of True North.

the proposed dive time. Then add this to the charted depth. When you are at the dive site you can check your calculations by using a weighted rope or an echo sounder.

○ *Tides* While tide tables indicate the times of high and low water, charts include a table of figures which give the direction of the tidal stream, and its speed in knots at Springs and Neaps. The key to the speed and direction lies in a diamond on the chart nearest to your dive site. In the diamond is a capital letter which relates to a table of figures, also shown on the chart. The table may show that at high water the speed of the tidal stream is 0.8 knots and the direction it is flowing *towards* is 090 magnetic. Winds come *from* the compass bearing, tides go *towards* it. Note that the current is usually greater off headlands and less in sheltered bays.

## Transits

If you discover a good dive site — perhaps one with a wreck — it is useful to record exactly where it is. This can be done by taking transits. A transit is made by choosing two distinctive landmarks, say a large tree and a church, which are lined up one in front of the other when you are at the location you wish to record. Besides marking your own transits, it is also useful to understand those made by other divers, so you can re-locate sites they have found.

The cheapest ways are often the most appropriate. When you are at the point you want to record, use a compass to take bearings from at least two conspicuous landmarks some distance apart (see diagram). Note down the bearings or mark them on the chart. To find the position again, head out along one

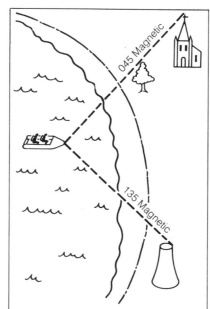

Transits. When using a compass take a bearing, line up the rotating bezel with Magnetic North, and note the bearings of at least two distinctive landmarks. This will enable you to locate the same position at a future date.

of the bearings and when it lines up with the other, you will have reached the site. Avoid choosing bearings which intersect at very acute or obtuse angles, as this will make it more difficult to obtain an accurate reading.

## Search procedure

Any underwater search is usually a lengthy procedure and can be a frustrating and fruitless exercise if it is not carried out systematically. Searching a large area for a single anchor or mislaid snorkel is generally impractical. Narrow down

the area of search as much as possible by trying to find out where the object *should* be according to the person who lost it or a local fisherman who knows where a particular wreck is. If he can give bearings, so much the better.

Consider, too, the effects of the tide or current which may carry an object some distance from where it was dropped. An echo sounder can help pinpoint a wreck by indicating a sudden change in depth, but it cannot distinguish between wrecks and rocks.

Because of the needle-in-a-haystack nature of the operation it is more likely to be successful if a team of divers comb an area together. This requires careful planning and co-ordination, and can be approached in several ways:

### (a) Free-line search

The search area is outlined using weighted lines attached to buoys. Divers hold a free-line or swim-line and spread out along one edge of the search area. The distance between divers depends on the visibility; there should be an overlap in the range of each diver's visibility.

Once in position the divers move forwards together and if a find is made it is tagged using a surface marker buoy which each diver is towing.

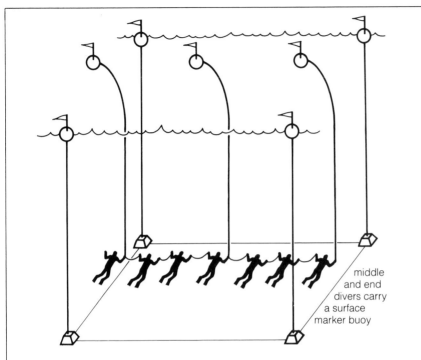

Free-line search. Divers hold the line and move forwards together. They are close enough to be able to see the entire area between them.

middle and end divers carry a surface marker buoy

## (b) Fixed line search

This method is suitable when visibility is poor. Two parallel lines of conspicuous material, such as white or day-glow tape, are laid down and fixed on the sea-bed. A line, weighted at each end, is then placed across the ends of the parallel lines (see diagram). Two divers swim towards each other on either side of the adjoining line, scanning the sea floor as they go. When they reach the weight at the other end they move the line along, turn around and repeat the procedure.

## (c) Circular search

The circular search involves just one diver and one shot-line. The

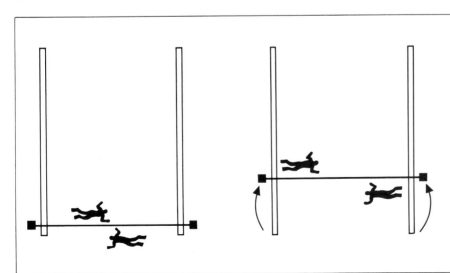

Fixed line search. This method is appropriate when visibility is poor. Two parallel lines of conspicuous material, such as white or day-glow tape, are laid down and fixed to the sea bed. A line, weighted at each end, is then placed across the ends of the parallel lines. Two divers swim towards each other on either side of the weighted line, scanning the sea floor as they go. When they reach the weight at the other end they move the line along and repeat the procedure.

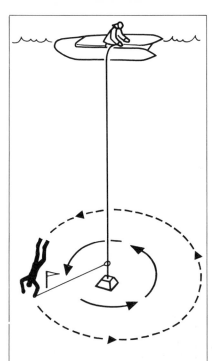

A circular search involves just one diver, surface cover and a single weighted line. The diver attaches a 'distance line' to the shot line and swims around it, keeping the distance line taut. He marks the beginning of his circular swim, and when he returns to the mark he lets out some rope so that his next circuit has a bigger radius.

diver attaches a 'distance line' to the shot-line and swims around it keeping the distance line taut. He marks the beginning of the circular swim and when he returns to the mark he lets out some rope so that his next circuit has a bigger radius.

## Marine salvage

If you are fortunate enough to stumble across an uncharted wreck, she may have high salvage

value and be worth marking with a buoy and taking a bearing of the location.

Before you can make a bid for legal salvaging of the wreck you must first establish her identity and track down the owner. This calls for detective work and a degree of luck. Some indication of the ship's identity may be found on the wreck — name plates, distinctive cargo, etc. Further clues can be gleaned from local fishermen, harbour officials and back issues of local newspapers. Shipping organisations and maritime museums also have records of wrecks and may prove a useful source of information.

Once the identity of the wreck is established the owner can often be traced via the insurance company which processed the claim. The owner will either charge a flat sum for the wreck depending on its value to him, or he will offer you a percentage of the value of the booty.

Small items can be raised using buoyancy bags, old oil drums or buckets filled from spare air cylinders. Remember that the rate of ascent will increase as the air expands near the surface. This can be controlled by spilling air from the lifting bags or buckets during the ascent. If control is lost, the air containers might hit the surface so violently that they turn upside down

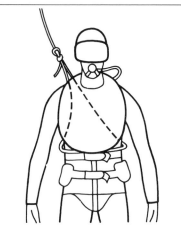

Roped diving. The rope should be looped beneath the diver's arms and tied in a bowline behind his neck. It must pass under the equipment in case the weightbelt or aqualung has to be jettisoned in an emergency.

and immediately lose their buoyancy.

Recovering larger objects requires specialist skills and equipment which may include underwater cutting techniques and explosives, beyond the scope of normal sport diving.

## Roped diving

When diving in poor visibility or in a confined area, such as in a wreck, a diver should be in direct contact with the surface via a life line or signal line. The line is looped under the diver's arms and tied with a bowline behind his neck. It must go under his weightbelt and aqualung in case they have to be jettisoned in an emergency.

The person on the surface in charge of the other end of the line must be an experienced diver who understands line signals. He must be attentive the whole time the roped diver is in the water and keep the line taut so that signals can be given easily.

If no response is given to a signal from the surface it should be repeated, giving time for the diver to reply. If there is still no response a standby diver should immediately be sent down.

## Line signals

In order to communicate when you cannot see the other person, a series of line signals has been developed. These may be used between two divers linked by a buddy line, or between the surface attendant and a diver.

| | | |
|---|---|---|
| *One pull* | Are you OK? | I'm OK |
| *Two pulls* | Stay where you are | I'm staying here |
| *Three pulls* | Go down | I'm going down |
| (buddy line) | Move away | |
| *Four pulls* | Come up | I'm coming up |
| (buddy line) | Come to me | |

## Marine archaeology

If you come across an archaeological site underwater, take bearings and/or mark the site with a buoy. Then inform the appropriate governing body or association. Do not plunder artifacts from the site as you may be destroying evidence of great importance to archaeological research, as well as breaking the law.

Before the site is disturbed, it is surveyed and notes, sketches and photographs are taken. Each photograph should include a black and white rod with an arrow at one end pointing to Magnetic North.

Excavating a site is a slow process as sand and silt are carefully sifted to minimise damage. It generally involves hours of exacting, painstaking work, which may mean very little until all the findings are pieced together to reveal the overall picture.

When it is brought to the surface, each item is carefully treated to prevent deterioration, which may accelerate in air. Tapping with a hammer should remove large concretions, while a bath of 10% nitric acid will clean off finer particles and growths. Glass, leather, wood and bone can be preserved in distilled water once the salt water has been thoroughly washed off.

It may be possible to join an excavation team. In some countries regular courses are held, teaching techniques of underwater archaeology and conservation of artifacts.

## Marine biology

Just as the study of plants and animals on land is a vast subject, marine biology covers a wide field. If you plan to investigate the topic in greater detail than the usual casual observation and identification, it will be more manageable if you choose one main area and seek out specialist books on the subject.

As on land, the various forms of sea life thrive in different environments. Within these habitats they compete with other organisms for light, space and food. Many unusual relationships have been established between plants and animals, and between different species of plants or animals. Many divers find studying the behaviour of marine life more rewarding than simply recording each new variety they see.

Try to limit the number of samples you bring to the surface. Instead, rely mainly on notes, sketches and photographs, which can later be transferred into a book or file. On an underwater slate, record such details as the date,

Studying marine life can be very rewarding.

## Underwater photography

By taking photographs underwater you not only create a vivid visual record of your dives, but you can begin to show friends concrete evidence of why you find diving so fascinating.

Before you can treat underwater photography seriously, you must first be at home underwater. You cannot concentrate on taking pictures when you are worried about your diving gear. You must also agree with your buddy on photography's place in the dive plan.

dive site, depth, terrain, flora and fauna, the colour, size and behaviour of the specimen which interests you.

The simplest underwater housing for a camera is a waterproof plastic bag with built-in gloves which enable you to operate the controls.

### Types of camera

If you want to take the camera beneath the surface, you need a special underwater housing or underwater camera. The cheapest underwater cameras are the 110mm models. These are small, light and robust, with built-in flash. Although models vary, these cameras may be waterproof to only 5m. They are ideal for beginners who want to take holiday snaps, but the picture quality is often disappointing.

The 35mm Nikonos is the underwater camera most widely used by divers. It is no larger than an ordinary 35mm single lens reflex camera, it is easy to operate and can give good results.

Alternatively, you can get an underwater housing for most land cameras. This is a watertight container with large control knobs which link in with the focusing and aperture rings, as well as shutter release and film advance mechanism. Commercial makes are available for 110, 35mm reflex, non-reflex and roll film cameras.

When wearing a mask it is impossible to put your eye close to the viewfinder so you can see everything that will appear in the

The nice thing about underwater photography is that it can be approached at any level; it offers opportunities for amateurs and professionals alike. It is possible to take satisfactory photos or movie film with an ordinary land camera through the 'window' of a glass bottom boat, or even glass bottom bucket. If the sun is shining on the subject and if the glass is fairly clean, the pictures will be bright and clear. But be careful whenever you take a land camera near the sea; water upsets the electrics and salt causes corrosion.

Nikonos V underwater camera.

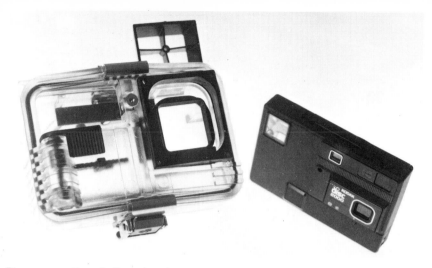

Disc camera with an Ikelite underwater housing.

Ikelite underwater housing for a single lens reflex camera. The housing has been opened into its two halves, and the camera mounted on the housing back.

prism, called a Sportsfinder or Actionfinder.

Whatever you choose, remember that the eye for a good picture and knowing the limitations of the camera are more important than how much you paid for the equipment. An expensive camera may increase the *potential* for good pictures, but it does not guarantee the results.

**Effects of water**

The biggest problem in underwater photography is the water itself. In water, objects appear closer than they really are, and a 35mm wideangle lens underwater is approximately equivalent to a standard 50mm lens on land. This is because light is refracted, or bent, when it passes from the medium of water into the air behind the front element of the lens or housing. As a result, the top of an object seems higher and the bottom seems lower, making it appear larger and therefore nearer. Fortunately, the camera 'sees' the object just as a diver wearing a mask sees it. If it *appears* to be 2m away, set the focusing ring to 2m. Do not measure the actual distance, unless you have a camera with correcting optics. This involves a dome port which enables the light to pass from the water to the air behind the port at right angles. Light passing through

picture. A plastic frame can be fitted to the top of some cameras to help you line up the shot. Certain land cameras have pentaprisms which can be replaced by a larger

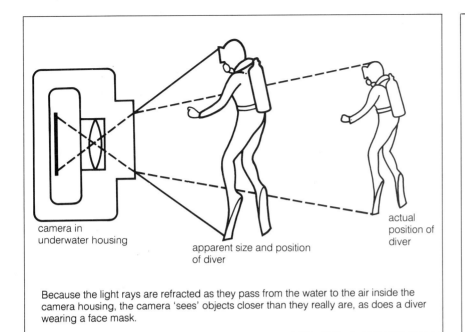

Because the light rays are refracted as they pass from the water to the air inside the camera housing, the camera 'sees' objects closer than they really are, as does a diver wearing a face mask.

camera in
underwater housing

apparent size and position
of diver

actual
position of
diver

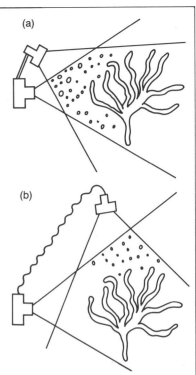

The light from a flashgun illuminates any particles floating in the water. (a) If the flashgun is positioned near the camera it will light up most of the particles between the lens and the subject, causing loss of quality and contrast. (b) If the flashgun is positioned well away from the camera at an angle to it the number of illuminated particles will be reduced.

the port at right angles will not be refracted.

Water also creates problems because of suspended marine organisms and sand particles that reduce visibility and diffuse the light. For a photograph which includes a whole diver, using a 35mm lens, the camera needs to be about 2m away. That is 2m of particle-laden water between the film and the subject of the picture. As a rule of thumb, the camera-to-subject distance should not exceed a quarter of the visibility. So if the visibility is 4m, you should restrict yourself to taking subjects up to one metre from the lens.

A wider lens, say 15mm, is more expensive, but does enable you to move in much closer to the subject and so eliminate much of the water

between camera and subject.

By putting on a close-up lens or an extension tube for macro, you can obtain good close-up shots when visibility is less than about 1m.

When the sun is shining through the surface layers of water, you can obtain good results down to about 2m without using flash if visibility is good. If the surface is calm more light will pass through, rather than being broken up by the waves. But as you go deeper below the surface, more and more light is filtered out by the water. Not only does it get darker, but different colours are absorbed at different rates. Within the first 5m all the reds are filtered out of the ambient light, and red coral appears black. Orange appears black within 10m,

yellow will be completely absorbed by 20m, and green by 25m. Although colour correction filters can be used to correct the colour balance, they cut out more light, and are impractical deeper than about 3m. For clear results at depth, flash is needed to provide enough light to take the picture *and* to restore the true colours. Without

Near the surface successful photos can be taken without using flash.

Record the subject in a more interesting light by positioning the flashgun away from the camera.

flash the results would be blue/green.

Normally the best results are obtained by shooting in sunlight or by using flash. In these cases there is no need to choose a fast film, because the sun or flash will provide all the light you need. A film with a speed between 50 and 100 ASA/ISO should produce the best results.

A smaller aperture (larger f stop) gives a greater depth of field, which usually means that more of the picture will be sharp. Choose a slow shutter speed of 1/60th or 1/30th second to allow you to use a smaller aperture setting. If using flash, there will be an indication on the camera what shutter speed should be used.

Instead of using the flash gun mounted close to the camera, place it at arm's length away, or further. This gives a better modelling light to the subject, and also reduces the number of particles which are illuminated by the flash light (see diagram on p. 133).

### Plans and preparation
Before taking underwater camera gear to some exotic location, test it out in the swimming pool in time to see the results before you go away.

Have a fairly good idea of what you want to achieve *before* you go into the water. Plan the shots rather than shooting haphazardly. You

Natural light does interesting things underwater and an observant photographer will catch them on film.

cannot change lenses underwater. If you notice something which calls for a different lens, you have to get out of the water to change the lens, unless of course you have several underwater cameras each with different lenses.

## Choosing a subject

Even with inexpensive equipment it is possible to record interesting effects simply by looking at what is naturally around you. Light behaves beautifully underwater, with rays bursting through the water in a spectacular way, especially around silhouettes. Try to catch reflections on the surface by looking up at the sky through the water.

The best pictures are usually simple and clear. First, select your subject — an attractive piece of coral, or your buddy. Then position yourself to show it off to its best advantage, without too many distractions in the picture — perhaps against the dark blue of deep water, or with the sky as a backdrop.

When photographing fish and other sea creatures, be ready, be patient and move slowly. It is often better to sit and wait for them to come to you, than to charge around scaring them away. Taking down pieces of bread, or breaking up a sea urchin, is a great way of encouraging camera-shy fish to

perform for you.

Make sure the flash is charged up (if used). Check the exposure and the focus, unless the camera is automatic. And if you are not sure about the exposure, take several shots of the same subject using different settings. The expense of the extra film is minimal compared with the effort and expense of getting into the water.

## Maintenance

As with your dive gear, the more care you take of your camera equipment, the longer it will last. After diving in the sea, rinse everything thoroughly in fresh water. Dried salt can have a severe abrasive effect on the equipment.

'O' rings are used to provide the seals to keep the water out of the underwater camera or flashgun. To keep the ring supple, silicone grease is applied to it before the unit is put together. This attracts sand and grit, which prevent the 'O' ring from making a good seal. Especially when under pressure, water will enter through the gap and flood the camera. Clean the equipment very carefully when assembling it; underwater camera gear needs more attention than land cameras.

Good pictures are often the result of patient waiting for the right subject to swim into view.

## Camera equipment checklist

○ camera
○ housing (if used)
○ flash gun
○ spare batteries
○ film
○ filters
○ silicone grease
○ spare 'O' rings
○ small screwdriver
○ pair of pliers

Expect a high failure rate at first, though with a little care and planning you will soon be taking some very special holiday snaps.

# 9. Diving around the world

The world is full of exciting, intriguing and spectacular places to dive. Your log book or C card (certification card) is your passport to these aquatic delights, while your diving gear provides the life-support system which enables you to visit them.

Taking a package tour put together by a specialist operator might be the simplest and cheapest way to dive in exotic locations. The operators know the best dive sites around the world and can arrange special deals with airlines, hotels and dive centres.

On airlines, do not carry a dive knife in hand lugguage — airport security will not like it! Pack your ABLJ cylinder empty, with the valve left open. And place the depth gauge in an airtight container to prevent the reduced pressure damaging the mechanism.

Avoid travelling with excess weight, especially on planes. Leave certain items behind, and hire equipment from a dive centre abroad. This may be a diving outfit attached to a hotel or an independent specialist dive operator.

Because you *know* your own equipment is in good condition and fits you, it is best to take your regulator, lifejacket, diving suit (if needed), knife, watch, depth gauge, torch, compass, mask and possibly fins. Unless you are going

on an expedition to remote locations, do not burden yourself with weights or the large cylinder. When hiring dive gear, do not assume that it is well maintained. Check that it is in test and in good working order.

If you are diving with new people, find out how experienced they are and go through the signals and safety procedures with them. Ask which dive tables are being used and make sure you are happy with the planned bottom time and decompression stops (if made). Find out, too, if there are any special conditions or local hazards you should know about. For the location of recompression chambers in the country where you plan to dive, contact the tour operator or appropriate governing body (see Appendix 3).

## Where to go

If you have your own compressor, transport and enough finance, you can dive just about anywhere from the Arctic Circle to the remote islands of the Pacific Ocean. Without a compressor, you are restricted to areas which have a dive centre. But this is not such a great limitation, as dive centres naturally gravitate towards the best dive locations.

The following is a subjective catalogue of diving venues around

the world. It does not claim to be a comprehensive list and should be viewed simply as a starting point.

### North America
Between the sub-tropical seas in the South to the icy waters of the North, there is a wide range of diving opportunities in and around North America. Besides the Great Lakes, there are many freshwater lakes suitable for diving, especially in Wisconsin, New York State and Florida. Off the east coast there are numerous accessible wrecks between Charleston and Boston.

*The Florida Keys* offer boat dives, in water over 22°C (72°F), often with good visibility and abundant marine life.

*Hawaii*'s volcanoes have produced dramatic caves and drop-offs in water which is over 20°C (68°F) and generally clear. Beach and boat dives are available; some shallow sites are suitable for novices.

*The Gulf of California* provides an opportunity to dive with sea lions, grey whales and huge mantas. The water is warm, especially towards the south and facilities are good.

*The Cocos Islands*, off the west coast of Panama, offer some superb diving.

### The Caribbean
Throughout the Caribbean, the water is warm (over 22°C, 72°F),

visibility is usually good and the coral and fish life are good in specific locations.

*Barbados* has both beach and boat dives which offer an abundance of sea life, wrecks and good visibility.

*Bonaire*'s west coast has a beautiful coral reef with many dive sites, often accessible from the beach. Dive facilities are excellent.

*The Cayman Islands* offer first class diving with plenty to see in clear water, accessible from the beach or boat. Grand Cayman has excellent facilities and provides a suitable location for beginners or advanced divers.

*Cozumel* is situated just off Mexico's Yucatan peninsula. Divers are very well catered for, with many impressive beach and boat dives from the south and west coast.

*Cuba*'s Island of Pines, off the south coast offers some great opportunities, with well organised dive boats, and superb wreck and wall dives.

*Jamaica* has some dramatic drop-offs and coral gardens, especially along the north coast and off the western end of the island. There are sites suitable for either novice or advanced divers.

*St Lucia* is rich is sea life and has a sheer, coral-encrusted wall extending down from the Pitons.

Both the *US* and *British Virgin Islands* have some spectacular

dive sites, although facilities are better in the US Virgin Islands. These reef-fringed volcanic islands are ideal for beginners because of the shallow water, good visibility and abundance of marine life.

*Venezuela*'s Caribbean coastline offers some superb and virtually undived sites, especially around the islands of Los Roques and Las Aves.

## The Bahamas

The 700 islands of the Bahamas lie in the warm Gulf Stream, which keeps the water temperature over 24°C (75°F). Several good dive centres operate from different islands, and offer a wide range of diving experiences, including drift dives, spectacular drop-offs and enchanting coral gardens.

## Europe

*Britain* is extremely well equipped with dive facilities, considering it lies in temperate waters, which rarely exceed 16°C (60°F) in summer. Visibility ranges from about 1m to 15m (3ft to 50ft), and tidal currents in certain locations are dangerous. Novice divers should be under strict supervision.

Numerous wrecks litter the coastline, providing exciting challenges for the more experienced diver. Marine life can be abundant, including wrasse, mullet, flatfish, crab, lobster,

Gorgonian coral and kelp beds. The more popular dives are found along the west and south coasts, especially off the Scilly Isles, as well as in freshwater quarries inland.

*The Azores* has interesting underwater caves and canyons accessible by boat, as well as some of the larger Atlantic fish, such as grouper, barracuda and rays.

*The Canary Islands*, in the Atlantic and off the coast of Morocco, have dive centres on a number of islands, the most popular of which is Lanzarote.

*Madeira*, also off the coast of Morocco, has several underwater caves, drop-offs and a couple of wrecks. The area is rich in marine life because it is washed by the warm Gulf Stream.

*Norway*'s fiorded coastline offers spectacular, deep, clear-water diving, but scant marine life.

*The Mediterranean* generally has warm, clear water, though the fish stocks have been seriously depleted because of over-fishing.

*Crete* offers dive holidays which are free from the restrictions often imposed to protect the archaeological sites in the waters around Greece.

*Corfu* has some steep drop-offs and, on the west coast, interesting underwater caves, reached by boat.

*Cyprus* has some very good

In the Bahamas the Underwater Explorers Society (Unexso) runs an efficient dive operation.

diving, backed by excellent facilities.

*France* has a number of dive centres along its varied south coast, with many good dive sites. Diving in France is very popular and well organised.

*Italy* is a keen diving nation, but Italian waters have largely been fished out through over-zealous spear fishing.

*Malta* and *Gozo* have very good facilities for the diver and some of the best diving in the Mediterranean, suitable for either the inexperienced or more proficient diver.

*Spain*'s Costa Brava offers some good diving, especially around the Islas de Medas. It is suitable for beginners and experienced divers, with some shallow dives as well as

deeper dives through caverns and tunnels. The Balearic Islands also have good diving possibilities.

## The Red Sea
For some time the Red Sea has provided a strong magnet for divers of all standards. The water is warm (19 - 24°C, 67 - 75°F), visibility is generally excellent and dive facilities are well developed. Live-on-board boats and shore dives reveal a spectacular underwater environment, with a visual feast of fish and coral. The most popular dive sites are located along the east coast of the Sinai Desert, developed by the Israelis, but now in Egyptian hands. Eilat, at the northern end of the Gulf of Eilat/Aqaba, is still in Israel and is the centre of a number of dive operations. As there are no recompression chambers in the

area, decompression dives should be avoided.

Across the border to the east of Eilat is Aqaba in Jordan. Facilities here are improving and the diving itself is excellent.

*The Sudan* offers striking underwater sights, with coral reefs, wrecks and some of the larger fish, including sharks and manta rays. Facilities are very basic, but worth the discomfort.

## Indian Ocean
Like the Caribbean and the Red Sea, the waters of the Indian Ocean are warm (21 - 27°C, 71 - 80°F), and generally clear with abundant marine life.

*Kenya*'s east coast has an underwater reserve where the marine life is protected and therefore flourishes. Good dive facilities exist, with scope for the beginner and experienced diver.

*The Maldives* are a string of 1,500 coral atolls situated to the south-west of India. Fringing reefs, only a metre or so deep, end in drop-offs which extend to beyond the limit of sport diving. There are good facilities for divers.

*Mauritius*, off the east coast of Madagascar, is the tip of an extinct volcano. Barrier reefs which protect the beaches have dangerous currents, sharks and many wrecks; they are only suitable for more experienced divers. Safer diving exists inside the reef, with plenty of marine life.

*The Seychelles*, to the north of Madagascar, have a dive resort on the main island, Mahe. Beach and boat dives are suitable for novices, while longer boat trips reach the more dramatic dive sites with drop-offs and extensive coral reefs.

*Sri Lanka*, just off the tip of India, is fringed by rich coral reefs. They are ideal for beginners and often accessible from the beach. Beyond the reefs lie the more dramatic drop-offs for more experienced divers.

### The Far East
*Malaysia* and *Sulawesi* are developing their diving facilities in response to a growing demand from visiting divers wishing to explore the superb diving potential.

*Palau*, east of the Philippines, is a collection of small islands set in a rich bed of exotic corals. Dive facilities are limited, but growing.

*The Philippines* comprise over 7,000 islands surrounded by coral reefs, which can be reached by boat. Some dive facilities do exist, with sites suitable for beginners and advanced divers, though much of the underwater realm remains unexplored.

*Truk Lagoon* in Micronesia contains numerous wrecks of Japanese planes and ships destroyed during World War II.

Dive facilities there are improving, giving the diver access to a fascinating, if gruesome, aquatic graveyard.

### Australia
The Great Barrier Reef, off the north-east coast of Australia, is 2,000km long and 30 to 50km wide. It boasts some of the most spectacular diving in the world. The Outer Reef and the Coral Sea are inhabited by many of the world's biggest sea creatures, while other reefs along the chain have, perhaps, the highest concentration of marine life to be found anywhere. Yet recent assaults by coral-eating crown of thorns starfish have denuded many areas of the reef.

To reach one of the 2,500 reefs in the chain, you must take boat, sea plane or helicopter. Live-aboard dive boats operate one- or two-week charters which enable you to dive the less accessible and unexplored areas. Diving is offered on a number of islands, though Heron Island, towards the southern end of the reef, has the most well-established dive operation.

In South Australia, Kangaroo Island is a short flight or boat trip from Adelaide. Besides the many wrecks, there is a seal sanctuary and unique underwater rock formations.

Sink holes in Mount Gambier, on the border of Victoria and South Australia, offer stunning cave diving, while the west coast of Victoria, Tasmania and the Bass Strait islands have hundreds of wrecks, some dating back to the seventeenth century.

### New Zealand
Off the east coast of the north island of New Zealand, the area called the Poor Knights offers almost everything a diver could wish for. Excellent visibility takes you down 30m through a cathedral-like archway inhabited by large jack fish. Well-organised dive boats operate from Tutukaka near the Bay of Islands. Water temperature peaks at about 20°C (68°F) in February and never falls below 16°C (60°F).

# Appendix 1

## Conversion tables

1 atmosphere = 10.07 metres sea water
33.05 feet sea water
10.34 metres fresh water
33.95 feet fresh water
1.033 kg per sq. cm
14.7 lb per sq. in

1 metre = 39.37 inches
3.281 feet
0.5468 fathoms

1 fathom = 1.823 metres

1 nautical mile = 1.853 kilometres
6080 feet

1 lb per sq. in = 0.07 kg per sq. cm

1 kg per sq. cm = 14.223 lb per sq. in

| Cylinder capacity | | | Mass of air | |
|---|---|---|---|---|
| Cubic feet | Litres | Cubic metres | Pounds | Kilogrammes |
| 40 | 1133 | 1.133 | 3.1 | 1.39 |
| 45 | 1274 | 1.274 | 3.4 | 1.56 |
| 50 | 1416 | 1.416 | 3.8 | 1.74 |
| 55 | 1557 | 1.557 | 4.2 | 1.91 |
| 60 | 1699 | 1.699 | 4.6 | 2.08 |
| 65 | 1841 | 1.841 | 5.0 | 2.26 |
| 70 | 1982 | 1.982 | 5.2 | 2.26 |
| 75 | 2124 | 2.124 | 5.7 | 2.60 |
| 80 | 2265 | 2.265 | 6.1 | 2.78 |

# Appendix 2

## Beaufort scale

| Beaufort scale number | Description of wind | Effects of wind on land | Speed in knots |
|---|---|---|---|
| 0 | Calm | Smoke rises vertically. | Less than 1 |
| 1 | Light air | Smoke drifts, wind vanes do not move. | 1 - 3 |
| 2 | Light breeze | Wind felt on face, leaves rustle, wind vane moves. | 4 - 6 |
| 3 | Gentle breeze | Leaves and twigs move constantly, flags begin to move. | 7 - 10 |
| 4 | Moderate breeze | Raises dust and blows paper along. | 11 - 16 |
| 5 | Fresh breeze | Small trees sway, crested wavelets form on sheltered waters. | 17 - 21 |
| 6 | Strong breeze | Large branches move, telephone lines whistle. | 22 - 27 |
| 7 | Moderate gale | Whole trees move, hard to walk against the wind. | 28 - 33 |
| 8 | Fresh gale | Breaks twigs off trees. | 34 - 40 |
| 9 | Strong gale | Roof slates move, slight structural damage likely. | 41 - 47 |
| 10 | Whole gale | Trees uprooted, considerable structural damage. | 48 - 55 |
| 11 | Storm | Widespread structural damage. | 56 - 65 |
| 12 | Hurricane | Widespread devastation. | Over 65 |

# Appendix 3 Useful Addresses

**World Underwater Federation –** Confédération Mondiale des Activités Subaquatiques (CMAS), 34 rue du Colisée, 75008 Paris. Tel 225 60 42.

**Australia** Australian Underwater Federation, PO Box 56, Hampton, Victoria 3188, or 3 Victoria St, New Lambton NSW 2305, Australia. Tel 049 540379.

**Canada** Association of Canadian Underwater Councils, National Sport and Recreation Center, 333 River Road, Vanier City, Ontario K1L 8B9. Tel 613 746 579.

**New Zealand** New Zealand Underwater Association Inc, 3rd Floor, AA Mutual Building, Cnr O'Connell & Chancery Streets, Auckland 1, New Zealand. *Or* PO Box 875, Auckland, New Zealand. Tel 778629.

**South Africa** South African Underwater Union, PO Box 201, Rondesbosch, 7700, Cape Town, South Africa. Tel 021 69 85 31.

**The United Kingdom** British Sub-Aqua Club (BS-AC), 16 Upper Woburn Place, London WC1H 0QW. Tel (01) 387 9302. *And* The Sub-Aqua Association (SAA), 34 Buckingham Palace Road, London SW1 0QP. Tel 01 828 4551.

**USA** Professional Association of Diving Instructors (PADI), 1243 East Warner Avenue, Box 15550, Santa Ana, California 92705, USA. *And* National Association of Underwater Instructors (NAUI), PO Box 630, 785 Colton Avenue, Colton, California 92324, USA. Tel (714) 824 5440. *And* Underwater Society of America (USA), 732 50th Street, West Palm Beach, Florida 33407, USA. Tel (305) 844 1124. *And* National YMCA Center for Underwater Activities, PO Box 1547, Key West, Florida 33040, USA. Tel (305) 294 5288.

# Further reading

**Divers and diving** by Reg Vallintine, Blandford, 1981.

**Easy diving** by Lou Fead & Alan Watkinson, Underwater World Publications, 1985.

**Sport diving** The British Sub-Aqua Club Diving Manual, Stanley Paul, revised edition 1985.

**The pocket underwater diving** by Reg Vallintine, Bell & Hyman, 1985.

**The technique of underwater diving** by Peter Dick and David Sisman, vol. 1 Basic techniques, vol. 2 Advanced diving, Pelham Books, 1986.

# Glossary

'A' clamp The section of the regulator which attaches to the pillar valve of the cylinder.

'A' flag Blue and white International Code flag meaning 'Diver down, keep clear'.

Adjustable buoyancy lifejacket (ABLJ) A lifejacket incorporating a small cylinder of compressed air.

Air embolism One of three types of burst lung. In this case expanding air enters the bloodstream and forms bubbles.

Aqualung Underwater breathing apparatus including harness, compressed air cylinder and regulator.

Assisted ascent Two divers ascending together sharing air from one cylinder.

Atmosphere A unit of pressure equal to 14.7 lb per sq. in or 1 bar (the average pressure of air at sea level). Pressure underwater increases by 1 atmosphere for every 10m (33ft) of depth.

Bends Term used for decompression sickness.

Boot A heavy rubber cover which protects the base of the cylinder and enables it to stand upright.

Bottom time The interval of time between the beginning of the descent and the beginning of the ascent.

Buddy breathing System by which two divers share one regulator to breathe from one cylinder of air.

Buoyancy compensator (BC) A lifejacket which uses a direct feed line from the main cylinder and, sometimes, also a cartridge of carbon dioxide which can be inflated once only in an emergency at the surface.

Buoyant ascent A rapid emergency ascent following the inflation of a compressed air lifejacket.

Compressor Pump used to fill cylinders with compressed air.

Console A collection of gauges mounted together.

Contents gauge A dial which indicates the amount of air in the cylinder.

Controlled lift An emergency ascent in which an unconscious diver is brought to the surface while buoyancy is controlled by

releasing air from a lifejacket.

Decompression dive A dive which requires a decompression stop.

Decompression sickness Also called the bends. This condition which can be serious or even fatal is caused by the rapid release of pressure, making nitrogen in the blood and body tissues take the form of bubbles.

Decompression stop A halt near the surface made during the ascent to allow the nitrogen in the body to dissipate.

Decompression table A table of times and depths used to calculate the limits of safe diving.

Demand valve (DV) See regulator.

Depth gauge An instrument which shows the diver's depth beneath the surface.

Direct feed A hose which supplies air from the first stage of the regulator to the lifejacket. ·

Dive timer A timing device which is activated when it is submerged.

Ecosystem Animal and plant populations, and their relationships to one another and to their environment.

Emphysema The result of expanding air bursting out of the lung and entering the tissues between and above the lungs.

Fathom A unit of length used for measuring the depth of water. One fathom equals 1.8m (6ft).

Free ascent A dash to the surface in an emergency, breathing out all the way to try to avoid a burst lung.

Harness Straps, backpack and waist belt attached to the cylinder so it can be worn by the diver.

Hypothermia Condition of heat loss from the body, with a resulting drop in body temperature.

Knot Unit of speed used in sea and air navigation, equal to one nautical mile per hour (1.1508 mph on land) or 1.7 ft per sec.

Long john Part of a wet suit shaped like dungarees.

Mask squeeze Pressure on the face caused when the air trapped between the mask and the diver's face is compressed.

Mouthpiece Section of a snorkel or regulator which goes in the diver's mouth.

Nautical mile The length of one minute of arc measured along the meridian—in practice 1,853m (6,080ft).

Nitrogen narcosis Condition affecting divers' mental processes, apparently caused by the presence of too much nitrogen in their blood and body tissues. Also called the narcs. The effects increase with depth. They may begin soon after about 20m.

'O' ring A rubber washer used to form an airtight seal.

Octopus rig A spare second stage on a regulator, useful when sharing air.

Pillar valve The valve on the top of the cylinder onto which is attached the regulator.

Pneumothorax The result of expanding air bursting out of the lung and into the area between the lung and the chest wall. The lung usually collapses.

Purge button A section of the second stage of a regulator which can be pressed to release air through the mouthpiece.

Regulator Also called a demand valve (DV). A mechanism which reduces the pressure of the compressed air in the cylinder to the pressure of the surrounding water, so that it can be inhaled by the diver.

Residual nitrogen The absorbed nitrogen that remains in the diver's body after a dive. If his body contains excess nitrogen, he must leave a sufficient interval before diving again.

SCUBA Self-contained underwater breathing apparatus.

Second stage Section of the regulator which reduces the air pressure to ambient pressure so it can be breathed through the mouthpiece.

Shot line A weighted line marking an object on the sea-bed or providing a guide for divers during descent or ascent.

Surface lifejacket (SLJ) Jacket which does not use compressed air and is not suitable for divers.

Surface marker buoy (SMB) A floating buoy used by divers to mark their position.

# Index